I've travelled the world twice over,
Met the famous: saints and sinners,
Poets and artists, kings and queens,
Old stars and hopeful beginners,
I've been where no-one's been before,
Learned secrets from writers and cooks
All with one library ticket
To the wonderful world of books.

© JANICE JAMES.

LADY'S MEN

In April 1943, an American Liberator bomber, based in Lybia and christened by her crew *Lady Be Good*, vanished mysteriously. The crew were simply reported as 'Missing, presumed dead.' Then, fifteen years later, BP oilmen on an aerial reconnaissance over south-central Libya spotted the remains of the bomber four hundred and forty miles from its original destination. Examining in detail all the available evidence, Mario Martinez set out to discover what had really happened to the ill-fated craft and her crew.

MARIO MARTINEZ

◆

LADY'S MEN

The Saga of *Lady Be Good*
and her Crew
A haunting story of the
Second World War.

Complete and Unabridged

ULVERSCROFT
Leicester

First published in Great Britain in 1995 by
Leo Cooper, an imprint of
Pen & Sword Books Limited
Barnsley
Yorks

First Large Print Edition
published 1996
by arrangement with
Leo Cooper, an imprint of
Pen & Sword Books Limited
London

British Library CIP Data

Martinez, Mario
Lady's men: the saga of *Lady Be Good*
and her crew: a haunting story of the
Second World War.—Large print ed.—
Ulverscroft large print series: non-fiction
1. *Lady Be Good* (Ship) — History
2. World War, *1939 – 1945* — Aerial
operations, American 3. B-24 Bomber
4. Aircraft accidents — Libya — Investigation
I. Title
940.5′449′73

ISBN 0–7089–3555–9

Published by
F. A. Thorpe (Publishing) Ltd.
Anstey, Leicestershire
Set by Words & Graphics Ltd.
Anstey, Leicestershire
Printed and bound in Great Britain by
T. J. Press (Padstow) Ltd., Padstow, Cornwall

This book is printed on acid-free paper

Dedicated to those mostly forgotten flyers from the Second World War, living and dead, who served with their Liberator Bombers.

Acknowledgements

Numerous individuals helped with information or assisted in other ways before and during the writing of *Lady's Men*. Their names are listed in the section on Other Information Sources, along with related sources from which I drew further data such as military records, newspaper stories, magazines articles, museums, veterans' organizations and so on. In many cases these contributions date back ten years.

I must draw attention to a handful of people whose help was both special and indispensable. The exact details of how each one helped are too long to relate, but without their assistance *Lady's Men* would probably never have been written. The contributions of the following people, particularly those of the unwavering Messrs Martin, Bowerman and Hellewell, are acknowledged with deep and sincere thanks: Dr John Martin, Gordon Bowerman, Dr Don Sheridan,

Don Livingstone, Richard Byers, Edwin Gluck, Charles Hellewell, Richard Dahlstedt, Dennis McClendon, Len Morgan, and the late Elizabeth Betty Henry (sister of William Hatton) and her son, Paul Henry.

I would also like to thank Leo Cooper of Pen & Sword Books, who met me, listened to what I had to say, and without delay came to a positive decision regarding a new *Lady Be Good* book.

A Note About Times

Establishing the precise times at which certain events took place is critical in unravelling the mystery of *Lady Be Good*. But time can be expressed in three different ways: for example, on 4 April, 1943, Liberators numbers 73, 90 and 95 took off from Soluch virtually together at 1145 GMT; but local time used in Benghazi (which was that for Cairo) was GMT plus 2 hours, expressed as 1345 local time and also as 1.45 p.m. local. The military report dealing with the B-17s from Algeria (Headquarters Northwest African Air Forces) makes no mention of GMT, but it is assumed to be based on GMT as Algeria is close to the Greenwich meridian.

In assembling this book information has been drawn from a body of documents in which the hour is expressed in GMT as well as local time. In order not to confuse the reader, and in keeping with other known factors, different hours of the day or night are given as Benghazi local time unless expressly stated otherwise.

1

El Alamein

THE savage desert battle which brought the German and Italian land forces in North Africa to a halt, then began driving them west, was General Montgomery's victory at El Alamein. The battle began on 23 October, 1942, and finished on 2 November.

By and large the significance of the El Alamein victory was in the lift it gave to the Allies' morale. Winston Churchill said, 'Before Alamein we never had a victory. After Alamein we never had a defeat.' Churchill also later described the battle as 'the turning of the hinge of fate'. When it was over Field Marshal Erwin Rommel's Afrika Korps was virtually broken and on the run; broken by a skinny 55-year-old general, Bernard Montgomery. He had forced the younger but sick Rommel, the Desert Fox, to turn tail and flee.

Prior to El Alamein it was the British Eighth Army that was on the run. In March, 1942, Rommel defeated the British under General Wavell at El Agheila, and the Allies became concerned about the threat this posed to the Suez Canal. The Afrika Korps' reputation as a solid fighting machine was well known and respected, as was indeed Rommel himself. Rommel then advanced eastwards towards Gazala in Libya, so the Allies were justified in the belief that his push to capture the Suez Canal was in gear. From early 1942 until the middle of the year the immediately threatened positions leading to Suez were Gazala followed by Tobruk.

What the Allies did not know was that Herr Hitler considered North Africa something of a side-show, an opinion not shared by Rommel. Rommel spent parts of March and April meeting with Hitler planning the push for Tobruk, which was scheduled for May. While Rommel was away, the British Eighth Army Commander, General Ritchie, took the opportunity to develop the Gazala area for the purpose of attack and for the defence of Tobruk. It did little more than check the Fox: Tobruk fell to Rommel in June, 1942, as a result of which Rommel was promoted to the rank of field marshal on 27 June. From Tobruk Rommel advanced further east up to Egypt's El Alamein, where he was finally halted on 17 July and his Afrika Korps badly weakened by General Auchinleck, who had taken over command of the Eighth Army.

In London Auchinleck's victory passed virtually unnoticed. The attention of Churchill and his War Cabinet was firmly fixed on priorities in Europe, the Middle East and beyond. As for the desert struggle in North Africa, what the British government and its Allies needed was a total victory; a smashing, thundering victory, which the Cabinet felt was well beyond the abilities of the modest Claude Auchinleck to achieve.

These were the dark days of 1942, when little was going the Allies' way except for minor American thrusts in the Pacific. In the east the German army was grinding its way towards Moscow.

In naval warfare German submarines in the Atlantic were threatening to wipe out Allied shipping. In the Eastern and Pacific theatres of war, Burma, Singapore, the Philippines, Malaya, Hong Kong and a host of other places had either fallen to or were being threatened by the Japanese. America's General Douglas MacArthur had already given up his command in the Philippines and was now in Australia regrouping. Britain was almost on her knees from the hammering she was taking from Hitler's nightly bombing raids. Then, of course, there was the Western Desert, where the weakened but still dangerous Rommel stood at El Alamein, a threat to Alexandria, and particularly to the Suez Canal and the huge Middle East oilfields.

Against this background of growing Axis threat there arose a rumbling mood of discontent in Britain's Parliament; so much so, in fact, that Prime Minister Churchill had to survive a motion of censure. A growing number of MPs, to say nothing of the nation at large, did not like the way Churchill was conducting the war and were less than thrilled with the

British army in North Africa. The censure took place on 1 July, after Rommel had reached El Alamein. Churchill survived the motion, but Clement Attlee, the coalition government's Labour Deputy Prime Minister, accused him of winning every debate and losing every battle. Churchill realized that drastic steps were needed to sort out the disorder of the troops in the Western Desert, so in early August he flew to North Africa to implement a purge at the highest levels of command.

Within a week Churchill had appraised the situation, made up his mind as to what action to take, and fired off a no-nonsense dispatch to his Deputy Prime Minister on 6 August, 1942. In it he said that after lengthy consultations with Field Marshal Smuts, with the Chief of the Imperial General Staff and with Richard Casey, the Minister of State for the Middle East, he had come to the conclusion that drastic and quick changes were needed in the High Command. Churchill then went on to detail how he proposed the Middle East Command should be split in two: General Alexander would be made Commander-in-Chief in the Near East; his place in Operation Torch (the combined American and British landing in North Africa) would be taken by General Montgomery. Operating under Alexander, General Gott was to command the Eighth Army. Generals Corbett and Ramsden were to be relieved of their respective posts in the Middle East and the 30th Corps. General Dorman-Smith would also lose his job.

Churchill assured Attlee that Field Marshal Smuts and his staff, as well as the Minister of State, were in full agreement that the proposed changes were the right course of action to take and that they would impart a vigorous new impulse to the army and restore confidence, which at the moment was badly lacking. He would be grateful to Attlee and the War Cabinet if they would approve his proposed changes.

Later in August, and still in North Africa, Churchill sent another dispatch to Attlee saying that as matters formerly stood under the old regime, the army was treading a perilous path: reduced to bits and pieces, overtaken by confusion and uncertainty. The concept of retreat had crept into their thinking.

A day after Churchill's 6 August dispatch, General Gott, Eighth Army commander-designate, was shot down and killed while flying to Cairo. The second choice to command the Eighth Army had always been Montgomery. Churchill cabled London, Montgomery took the stage — and the rest is history. Rommel and his broken army fled west with Montgomery close behind.

At the time of El Alamein the United States had been at war with Germany, Italy and Japan for less than a year, so there was still much preparation to be done. And with shoulders back and head down, the country was buzzing. Uncle Sam was gearing up, harnessing his industrial might, mobilizing and training his military forces. The war had conveniently slotted in with the country's unwritten principle that the business of America was business, and business was indeed good. The nation's focus was on war and the tools with which to fight it. Wall Street could not have been happier: with money to be made all around, the war was a blessing which lanced the last of the Depression's boils.

During this 'gearing up' stage America was not totally inactive militarily, although throughout much of 1942 US actions were largely defensive. The few and far between American offensives in the Pacific were only tokens of what, would follow; actions intended more to pep-up the folks back home than to bring down the foe from the Rising Sun. Notable among these was a surprise attack on the Japanese mainland, which rattled the recipients and made them sit up and take notice. The blow was purely psychological. A task force built around the carrier *Hornet* reached within 600 miles of the Japanese coast on 18 April, 1942, and sixteen B-25 bombers under the command of Lieutenant-Colonel James H. Doolittle took off on a successful attack on Tokyo, other Japanese cities, and targets in southern Honshu. Later that year the tide of war in the Pacific would slowly begin shifting in favour of the Allies.

By the middle of 1942 a major US strategy was already in place. In

September, 1941, President Franklin D. Roosevelt had approved a document signed by the military chiefs of staff stipulating that in the event of world conflict involving the United States in both west and east, the defeat of Germany would take precedence over the Pacific war. This strategy endured throughout the war years, and a new agency was established to regulate it and co-ordinate efforts: the Combined British-American Chiefs of Staff.

It was agreed that America would enter the European theatre of war by way of Morocco and Algeria. The plan was that once the landing had been made (a joint American/British effort), and when the enemy had been defeated, the combined Allied forces in North Africa would strike into Europe through Italy, attacking what Winston Churchill called 'the soft underbelly of Europe'. This notion of a soft underbelly was an amazing underestimation of Italy's geological features because, from a land invasion point of view, Italy's landscape was anything but a soft touch. The country contains considerable rough mountain terrain; had it not been for Axis misjudgement of their priorities regarding troop and equipment deployment, the eventual Allied probe through southern Europe might very well have failed.

While still mobilizing, an important American effort to help with the North African campaign was an operation called the Halverson Project, one of the first US efforts to help its allies on a world-wide front. It consisted of flying B-24 Liberator bombers from America to Egypt to help defend the Suez Canal and, in conjunction with the RAF Middle East Command, provide a heavy bomber force for the support of the British Eighth Army in the Near East.

The slowly increasing US bomber force drifting in from America began to slip into North Africa by way of eastern Egypt. One such aircraft arrived in March, 1943; a US Liberator B-24D bomber number 1-24301. A few days later, probably in Benghazi in Libya, some person or ground crew named her *Lady Be Good*. Not long before Easter of that year, she and her young, inexperienced crew would fly their first combat mission to Naples. They would take off in a sandstorm, head out over the Mediterranean, and vanish.

2

The Characters Assemble

IN February, 1942, two B-24D Liberator heavy bombardment groups were flown from America to Fayid in Egypt: the 98th and 376th Bomb Groups. They were welcome additions to the US Ninth 'Desert' Air Force, which by then was operating in North Africa. After El Alamein, with German and Italian forces retreating, the 98th and 376th Bomb Groups started moving their Liberators west to airfields abandoned by the enemy.

By January, 1943, Montgomery had pushed Rommel back through Tripoli. Two months earlier the Americans had landed in Morocco and Algeria, and the British Long Range Desert Group had swept the Italians from Libya's southern desert. Now that the curtain was falling on Rommel in North Africa it became safe to move the Liberators west to the

Benghazi region of Libya, an area once captured, then lost, then captured again by the Allies.

By March the Ninth Air Force, under the command of Brigadier-General Uzal G. Ent, was fully operational in the Benghazi region. Their overall objective was to strike supply ports, railway marshalling yards, factories, bridges and airfields behind enemy lines. Their first targets would be Sicily and southern Italy, to quicken the cut-off of supplies to what remained of Axis troops in North Africa.

Commanded by 28-year-old Colonel Keith K. Compton, the 376th Bomb Group was known as the 'Liberandos' and would become the most decorated American bomb group of the Second World War. The group was composed of four squadrons: the 512th, 513th, 514th and 515th. With an average of six Liberators in each squadron, the number on call was usually 20 to 25 bombers, and they were often required to take off without fighter escort.

The 376th was stationed near the Libyan coast in the village of Soluch,

13

an area some 30 miles south of Benghazi, at a crude airfield bulldozed level out of sand. Soluch was hot and clammy, subject to sandstorms and many other discomforts. At dusk the temperature would suddenly drop, and after a rainstorm there was mud to contend with. Flyers and ground crews lived under tents; food and water were scarce. The men suffered from a variety of ailments, such as dysentery, diarrhoea, yellow jaundice, constipation and sore eyes. Among flyers one of the most common complaints was haemorrhoids. Mission briefings were held outdoors — in fact, almost everything was in the open, including latrines. Enemy fighter planes from nearby Crete were almost always a threat.

Tarpaulins covered the Liberators to protect them from sandstorms and cold nights. When their engines were started up, a hurricane of sand would blow for hundreds of yards behind and upward; men and bombers lived with the constant presence of this all-pervasive sand. The bombers drank gasoline mixed with sand; the men ate food and drank water mixed with more of the same. The sand gave the Liberators trouble with engines, oxygen and hydraulic lines, engine oil filters and instruments.

Manufactured by the Consolidated Aircraft Company, the Liberator bomber was powered by four 1,200 hp Pratt & Whitney engines, measured 66 feet long and 18 feet high, and fully loaded could take off with a gross weight of 65,000 lbs. Its maximum speed was 300 mph, and its range, subject to bomb load, was 4,600 miles. It had nine machine guns and could carry 8,000 lbs in bombs. Throughout the war the Liberator B-24's principal users were the United States, Great Britain, Canada and Australia. The Liberators' most famous single exploit, in which the 376th Bomb Group participated, was a daylight low-level raid on the Romanian oilfields at Ploesti on 1 August, 1943, when 177 of them took off from or near Benghazi and nearly one-third never returned.

Late in 1942 B-24D Liberator bombers in large numbers started rolling off the assembly line in San Diego, California. On 9 December one such group of bombers included Liberator number 1-24301. The number indicated that the bomber was the 24,301st aircraft to be ordered from industry by the American government during 1941. On 5 February, 1943, Liberator 1-24301 and several others were ferried from San Diego to Fort Worth, Texas, where they were groomed for the weather and combat conditions they would face at their destination. Ten days later the same Liberator and her sister ships were deemed ready for combat and flown from Fort Worth to Topeka in Kansas, where 1-24301 was assigned her first crew:

Second Lieutenant Samuel D. Rose, pilot

Second Lieutenant Ralph O. Grace, co-pilot

Second Lieutenant Millard B. Kesler, navigator

Second Lieutenant Charles H. Midgley, bombardier

Technical Sergeant William S. Nelson, engineer

Private Carl L. Valentine, radio operator

Private Joseph E. Maleski, assistant engineer

Staff Sergeant Allyn Leavy, assistant radio operator

Staff Sergeant Charles Marshall, gunner

Staff Sergeant Roscoe S. Hoover, tail gunner.

Her pilot, Sam Rose, a man with a flair for drawing, chalked the name *Bugs Buggy* near the bomber's nose. But his crew didn't like the sobriquet, so when the name was washed away by rain on a training flight over Kansas the brand-new Liberator was left anonymous. Sam Rose and Charles Midgley remember clearly to this day that the ship had no name when she left the States for combat. But an alternative view came from the late Millard Kesler, Rose's navigator, who claimed that a member of their crew suggested the name *Lady Be Good*.

On 8 March the Rose crew and six others started the journey to North Africa with their Liberators, travelling from Topeka to Florida, then Trinidad, Brazil, Ascension Island, the Ivory Coast, Nigeria, Sudan, and Cairo in Egypt. Rose and his crew were several days late getting away from Trinidad, thanks to Rose parking the ship too close to some trees and doing minor damage to a wing-tip. This had to be repaired and the crew then had to hustle to catch up with their fellow Liberators, who had pushed on to Brazil. They finally arrived at their destination, Soluch airfield, on 25 March, 1943.

New Liberators were badly needed in North Africa by Ninth Bomber Command. As soon as planes got there they would often be taken from the raw crews who had flown them in and given to more experienced flyers, men with combat missions already under their belts. In almost every case this would leave the newly-arrived crews without a Liberator. This was what happened to Sam Rose — his Liberator was taken away from him for a going-over and he never saw her again.

After her maintenance inspection, Liberator 1-24301 would be assigned to another crew:

First Lieutenant William J. Hatton, pilot

Second Lieutenant Robert F. Toner, co-pilot

Second Lieutenant Dp Hays, navigator

Second Lieutenant John S. Woravka, bombardier

Technical Sergeant Harold S. Ripslinger, flight engineer/gunner

Technical Sergeant Robert E. LaMotte, radio operator/gunner

Staff Sergeant Samuel E. Adams, tail gunner

Staff Sergeant Guy E. Shelley Jnr, waist gunner/assistant engineer

Staff Sergeant Vernon L. Moore, waist gunner/assistant radio operator.

According to previous accounts, other new Liberators arrived in Soluch along with 1-24301 on 25 March. This is probably true. What is not true is that the pilot of one of these Liberators was William Hatton. He and his crew had arrived prior to the Rose crew: they were already in Africa by 12 March, and certainly in Soluch by 18 March. In a letter to his parents dated Thursday, 18 March, 1943, Hatton wrote:

Things are settling down now, and are going surprisingly well for me. If there are times when you don't hear from me for quite a while, don't worry about it, since the mail takes a long time to come from the Middle East. It is very difficult to write because of the fact that the censor might cut something out, and with this on my mind there are lots of limitations.

The bomber Hatton flew from Topeka was 42-40081, probably named *Old Faithfull*. It is more than likely that this bomber was not given to another crew, but was flown from Soluch to Deversoir, north of Cairo, for examination and the repair of what was discovered to be a cracked engine cylinder. In the period 28 – 30 March, 1943, several members of Hatton's crew stayed in Deversoir with Liberator 42-40081: Sergeant Harold Ripslinger, probably Lieutenant Robert Toner, and perhaps Sergeant Guy Shelley. By the morning of 31 March the bomber still had not been repaired, however, so Ripslinger and his companions flew back to Soluch in another Liberator.

Irrespective of the date on which Bill Hatton and his crew arrived in Soluch, at some point between 25 March and 3 April an unknown person or crew not connected with either Rose, Hatton or their crews probably gave Liberator 1-24301 the name of *Lady Be Good*. It is the opinion of Sam Rose that the ship was named by a ground crew in North Africa, and that she was named not in Soluch but in Benghazi, where the aircraft was flown immediately after her arrival in Soluch from America. It has also been suggested that the Liberator was originally assigned to another air crew in Libya, and that this unknown crew christened her. This, perhaps having been the case, the bomber may then have been temporarily assigned to William Hatton and his crew on the day of Mission 109 while her normal crew, it is rumoured, were in Malta. Regardless of who thought of it, however, the name was painted on either side of the aircraft below and just forward of the cockpit.

'*Lady Be Good*' was the featured song and title of a popular 1941 musical film, roughly based on a 1925 George and Ira Gershwin stage musical of the same name. The song was written by Oscar Hammerstein II and Jerome Kern, and won the Academy Award for the best

21

song of 1941. The words of the song were most appropriate for the Liberator bomber which would bear its name:

Oh, *Lady Be Good*

Listen to my tale of woe,
It's terribly sad, but true.
All dressed up, no place to go,
Each evening I'm awfully blue.

I must win some winsome miss,
Can't go on like this,
I could blossom out, I know,
With somebody just like you, so,

Oh sweet and lovely *Lady Be Good*,
Oh *Lady Be Good* to me.
I'm so awfully misunderstood,
So *Lady Be Good* to me.
Oh please have some pity,
I'm all alone in this big city,
I tell you I'm just a lonesome babe
In the wood, so *Lady Be Good*
        to me.

After his arrival in Soluch, Hatton made a weather-aborted effort to participate in a mission as co-pilot with another crew piloted by First Lieutenant Richard F. Hurd, and flew several familiarization flights over Soluch and the sand dunes to its south with his own crew. Hatton and his men were then considered ready for combat. Their next flight would be the real thing. They need only wait now: wait for a mission, and for the Liberator in which to fly it. The mission was eventually scheduled for 4 April. At that time the German and Italian forces were on their last legs, bottled up in Tunisia; within a month they would be totally defeated. Hatton and his crew were to take part in Mission 109, a raid by 25 bombers on Naples harbour. They were assigned to *Lady Be Good*, which was to be part of Squadron 514 and given the number 64. Each bomber would have enough fuel for 12 hours' flying, carry between nine and twelve 500 lb bombs, and make the trip to Naples and back (1,600 – 1,700 miles including evasive action flying) in about nine or ten hours. But *Lady Be Good* was destined never to return to Soluch.

3

Doomed Crew

WHO were these men who boarded *Lady Be Good*, took off that April day, and then vanished, leaving in their wake a mystery? Where were they from? What were their backgrounds? What were they like?

The pilot, First Lieutenant William Hatton, was born in Jersey City, New Jersey, but was brought up in Whitestone, Long Island, Queens at 17 – 43 149th Street. A man with a Jesuit background, he attended Francis Xavier High School and then graduated from Fordham University, where he studied liberal arts and entertained thoughts of becoming a dentist. He was 26, five feet nine, weighed 160 lbs and had blondish hair. Hatton came from a comfortably-off family of Irish Catholic stock; one of eight children, he was the product of a happy home. He was a sensitive, caring and warm person.

After university in 1940, with war looming, he joined the US army's Ninth Regiment and was sent to Virginia Beach for training. He was released after one year on 1 December, 1941; but six days later Japan attacked Pearl Harbor and America entered the war. Less than happy with his foot-soldier days, Hatton joined the Army Air Corps at Mitchell Field, New York, where medical tests revealed spots on his lungs caused by sand from Virginia Beach the year before. After several weeks' treatment the spots cleared, but Hatton was understandably not fond of sand.

Hatton then trained on B-17 bombers in Florida at Hendrick's Field. Originally trained as a pursuit pilot, the decision to convert him into a bomber pilot was a mystery to him. In a letter to his mother in early August, 1942, written from the New Hotel Mayflower in Jacksonville, Florida, he said, 'By the way, Hendrick's Field is a bomber field and we don't know why they are sending us pursuit pilots to fly bombers. However, I guess they know what they're doing'. He looked forward to going overseas.

During his flight training days, in 1942, he married Amelia Jarsky, a local girl from his Whitestone home. In August, 1942, his sister, Elizabeth Henry, who had also just married and was honeymooning in Florida, visited Hatton at Hendrick's Field. During this visit William told his sister that he hoped never to be assigned to B-24s, as he felt they were hard planes from which to bail out.

Hatton's father, a publisher, was a stern but fair man who had lost an eye around 1940. He refused to let any of his children drive his new LaSalle car. When William informed him that he had been made commander of his own bomber, his father said, 'The world's gone crazy — but if the government will trust you with their bomber, I suppose you can drive my car.' Hatton was very much a homespun boy who wrote home frequently. The last letter he ever sent his parents was written on 27 March, 1943.

Richard Hurd was a friend of Hatton during his air force days:

Bill Hatton, pilot of *Lady Be Good*, was a good friend of mine, as we were together throughout much of our military flight training as aviation cadets. We then trained in B-17s before we were assigned to B-24s and the crews we both took overseas to North Africa and the 376th Bomb Group. I arrived at Soluch on 15 March, 1943, and flew my first combat mission on 23 March; I believe Bill Hatton and his crew arrived a few days later.

Having learned of Bill and his crew's arrival, I found I was being scheduled for the 2 April mission to Palermo, Sicily. Since I did not have a regular assigned co-pilot, and learning Bill was not assigned to a mission, I requested permission for Bill to fly with me — even though he was out of another squadron, the 514th, while I was a member of the 513th Squadron. But as the records show, the mission was a weather abort . . .

During our military flight training, Bill and I had an interesting experience. We had completed our first pilot training in B-17s and were assigned

Sunday Oct. 25th

Dear Mom,

Am finally settled at :
{ 39th Bombardment Group
Davis - Monthan Field,
Tucson, Arizona. }

Millie & I spent Thursday in Hollywood. We saw many stars & famous places and both of us enjoyed it fully. Bing Crosby posed specially for us and we are waiting for the snap-shot to be developed. Millie threatens to kill me if it doesn't turn out because I took it. *P.S. - Please send 2 wires & 1 prints now.* Love to you & Pop — From Both of us.

to the Second Air Force Headquarters at Salt Lake City, Utah. From there we were assigned to B-24s at Tucson, Arizona. Our travel to Tucson over a weekend gave sufficient time for a group of us, including Bill and his wife, to visit Hollywood in California. During our visit, Bill, his wife, myself and a couple of other officers were walking down one of the streets when we passed a bar bearing the sign 'Off Limits to Military Personnel'. One of the officers, a pilot named John Foster, looked in the open window and spotted Bing Crosby at the bar. He stepped in and asked Bing if he would step outside for a picture; Crosby very graciously obliged. I believe Bill's wife had a camera at the time.

I have learned that John Foster, after *Lady Be Good* was found, wrote to Bing Crosby and mentioned the episode of the picture-taking. He received a very nice personal letter in return from Bing, expressing his sorrow to Bill's wife. Though Crosby did not recall the date he did indicate the name of the bar he believed he was in at the time.

Bill Hatton was an easy-going man whose abilities as a pilot and leader were good but not exceptional. He was proud to be a pilot, although he still often referred to himself in letters to his mother as 'Your little Willie'. He was pleased to have Robert Toner as his co-pilot, for he thought Toner was a wonderful flyer; in fact, he felt Toner should have been pilot, not him.

Second Lieutenant Robert Toner, Hatton's co-pilot, was originally from Woonsocket, Rhode Island, but the family later moved to North Attleboro in Massachusetts. At 27, Toner was the oldest man in Hatton's crew and by far their most experienced flyer. He was a man of courage, determination and precision. A devout Catholic who seldom missed confession or mass, he was among the most religious of all the crew members, of whom probably five were Catholics. He spoke with a New England accent, something like John F. Kennedy. Toner was around five feet nine inches tall, weighed 165 lbs, and had a fair complexion with dark hair, perhaps a receding hairline. His address book displayed a list of lady friends; he also kept a regular diary.

Robert Toner experienced sorrow during his upbringing, having come from a broken home. He always wanted to fly aeroplanes, but was not a brilliant scholar and only achieved average grades. In 1940, prior to America's entry in the war, Toner tried to join the US Army Air Corps but was turned down because of his low school grades. He therefore went to Canada and joined the Royal Canadian Air Force, where he learned to fly and accumulated at least 200 hours at the controls. When America entered the war, Toner returned to the States and successfully reapplied for the Air Corps. Although accepted, he was made to learn to fly all over again, with the result that he was a highly-rated pilot with some 700 hours by the time be reached the 376th Bomb Group; he probably had several hundred more flying hours than William Hatton.

In one of his last letters home to his three sisters in Massachusetts, Toner wrote, 'You live day by day here and no future.'

Lady Be Good's navigator, Second Lieutenant Dp Hays, has been a much-discussed figure regarding his navigational abilities. His Mission 109 navigator's log was poorly filled in on the way to Naples, and virtually blank on the return leg. Some of the figures in his log are improperly listed, indicating a state of confusion and anxiety on the way to Naples. But in a letter to his parents dated 27 March, 1943, written from Soluch airfield, William Hatton says that Hays 'did a good job getting us over here from the States'.

Hays was a small man, only five feet six

Sat. March 27th

Dear Mom & Pop,

I had a few days off recently and went to Cairo. While there we visited the Pyramids and Sphinx and had pictures taken, which I'll send under separate cover.

The sight seeing was very interesting but I'll still take New York to any of all the cities I've yet seen. There is nothing truer than the old statement "there is no place like home."

Does Millie drop in on you as often as she used to? I hope everything is going well back there. As yet I have had no news about you folks at all.

A fellow just came in with the pictures that I mentioned above so I'll include a couple now. The fellow in the middle is Ray Walsh from Ohio and the little guys is 'Kay' Hays, my navigator. He did a good job in getting us over.

Too bad you can't see my "crew cut" under my hat.

That's all for now but more later.

Lots of love to all —

Your son,
Bill

inches tall and weighing 125 lbs. Born on 22 February, 1919, in Sedalia, Missouri, he has been described as looking totally out of place among his fellow crewmen. He has also been recalled as a man who probably never smiled; a Father Time figure who had a grey, albino-type look although he was only 24 at the time of Mission 109. Hays was probably balding on top, and his blond hair was long and greying at the sides. He was also a very heavy smoker. He was Protestant, but not particularly religious.

Hays started life off on the wrong foot, or at least a most unusual foot: he was never given a proper Christian name, just the two letters Dp. The crew called him Deep. A bank clerk in civilian life, Hays had attended junior college for two years and has been described as a man with few interests other than navigation. He joined the US Army Air Corps in January, 1942, and was commissioned in September of the same year.

George F. Coen knew Hays slightly:

I was a cadet in Dp Hays' class at Mather Field in 1942. We were in class 42-13, and I knew him casually. Later I flew in the storm of 4 April, 1943, in Algeria, the storm which resulted in the loss of *Lady Be Good* and her crew. I am convinced that Hays had the misfortune to encounter unexpected tail winds similar to those I experienced. Hays was a good man and deserved better luck . . .

I remember him as a quiet, likeable sort who was separated from me by several letters of the alphabet, so that I did not ever get very well acquainted with him. Further, the cadet days were a blur of feverish activity which is difficult to recall.

(Coen actually wrote 'the storm of 5 April, 1943', but no mission of any kind was flown from either Algeria or Libya that day because of heavy cloud cover over Italy. He clearly means 4 April, 1943.) Second Lieutenant John Woravka, *Lady Be Good*'s bombardier, was from Cleveland, Ohio. He was 26, five feet eight inches tall, and a man of burly build who was thick around the middle. He was most probably a Catholic. Robert

34

LaMotte, the radio operator, always called him 'Lefty', as on occasion did others in Hatton's crew. At some point just prior to or during Mission 109 Woravka cut the ring finger of his left hand and wrapped it with a Bandaid. The last message he sent his family was a cable from Africa to his brother Alex, saying 'please don't worry'.

Technical Sergeant Harold Ripslinger was Hatton's flight engineer/gunner. Ripslinger sprang from a large and very devout Catholic family in Saginaw, Michigan. One of his sisters was a Sister of Mercy nun and, like Toner and Hatton, he was a fervent Catholic who seldom missed mass; also like Toner, Ripslinger left a diary. A physically strong man, he had exceptional character and determination. He was 22 years old, five feet ten inches tall, weighed in at 180 lbs, and was inclined to use expressions like 'Oh boy'.

An outstanding athlete in high school, Ripslinger trained as a gunner with another crew member, Vernon Moore. He could not wait to go overseas, and once in Soluch was very keen that the crew's first combat mission should be a success. He had a pleasing personality and is described as a person who 'wore well', a direct, straight-talking, 'look-you-in-eye' type of man.

Ripslinger's diary for the six days prior to Mission 109, for part of which time he was sitting happily in Deversoir waiting for a Liberator to be repaired, gives some idea of his personality:

Monday 29 March
Still no plane. And still in town. Sleeping late in morning. Having nice showers and eating nice meals with lots of fruit.

Tuesday 30 March
Boy o' boy! What a vacation. Bet the boys at camp are really envious. Had cracked cylinder on engine. Saw a movie tonight. Swell!!!

Wednesday 31 March
Plane still not ready but came back in another B-24. The boys were glad to see us and vice versa. Nice trip.

Thursday 1 April
Nice sleep last nite. Got up too late for breakfast. Went to confession and

communion!!! Nice going Rip!! We are going to have mass every Thursday.

Friday 2 April

Nothing much doing today. Shelley and Sam got their first letters. Oh boy!!! Some got paid too. Mine was wrong. Won $45.00 in cards.

Saturday 3 April

Nothing exciting today. Sam got five letters. I'm waiting my first from Gert [Gertrude Taylor, his fiance]. Saw stage comedy tonight.

It is noticeable that Ripslinger's 3 April entry makes no mention of Mission 109, scheduled for the following day.

Lady Be Good's radio operator/gunner, Technical Sergeant Robert LaMotte, came from Lake Linden in Michigan. He too was a Catholic from a large family, having five brothers and one sister. Although 25, his looks were boyish: he was described as childlike in appearance, with a dark olive complexion and curly auburn hair. He was small in stature at five feet six inches, and light of weight at 130 lbs. LaMotte graduated from high school in 1936, and during the late Depression years worked for the Civilian Conservation Corporation. Like most people of his era, he probably never travelled far from home.

Staff Sergeant Samuel Adams, Hatton's tail gunner, was born in Speedwell, Kentucky, but grew up in Eureka in Illinois. A Protestant, Adams was 24, five feet seven inches tall, weighed 155 lbs, and had a fair complexion with brown hair and blue eyes. He and William Hatton were the only married crew members, and Adams was the only man with children — a son named Michael. A high school graduate, he was a house painter before the war, and like LaMotte had worked for the Civilian Conservation Corporation during the late Depression.

Adams was not an original member of Hatton's crew. In December, 1942, Hatton's original tail gunner allegedly went absent without leave; when he failed to return, Adams became his replacement. Coincidentally or deliberately, Adams was also elevated to the rank of staff sergeant on 1 January, 1943.

On 2 April, 1943, Adams and Guy Shelley became the first members of

Hatton's crew to receive letters from home after their arrival in Africa. The following day Adams received five more letters. There would have been much news for him from home, as his son had only recently been born.

Staff Sergeant Guy Shelley, the waist gunner/assistant engineer, was from Harrisburg in Pennsylvania. A Protestant, he was 26, five feet 11 inches tall and weighed 185 lbs. Both in the States and at Soluch he was fond of wearing a striped railroad engineer's cap, although it is unknown whether he had the cap with him during Mission 109. Vernon Moore, another *Lady Be Good* crew member, probably often kidded Shelley about this cap, saying that if trains didn't even stop at the coal town of Pittsburgh in Pennsylvania, what hope was there for a mere pimple of a place like Harrisburg. Powerfully built like Harold Ripslinger, Shelley was a man of extraordinary stamina and grit. He was the tallest and heaviest of the crew.

Staff Sergeant Vernon Moore, the waist gunner/assistant radio operator, was far and away the most enigmatic and casual member of the crew. He was from New Boston, Ohio, but he often spoke of being born in the same city as Roy Rogers, the cowboy film star, who had been born in Cincinnati. Moore was a great fan of Rogers and Western films. At 21 the youngest of the crew, he stood about five feet eight inches tall and weighed around 140 lbs. Next to Robert LaMotte, Moore was the youngest looking of the crew. He has been described as looking like a young Roddy McDowell.

Colleagues remember him as a reserved young man with hidden depths who seemed to be on the social fringes of his crew, more an observer than a participant; someone who would smile at something said in company, but was almost too shy to laugh out loud. Although neither lazy nor a fool he was extremely casual, to the extent of being careless about vital matters. A Protestant, at Christmas, 1942, Moore did not go home to his parents, but spent his leave with a lady friend.

Private Richard R. Dahlstedt was a member of the ground crew at Soluch airfield on 4 April, 1943. He remembers the crew of *Lady Be Good* well after meeting them in the mess tent the night before Mission 109:

On page 123 of Ivan Dimitri's book *Flights To Everywhere* is a picture of the mess tent where I met some of these boys. I had turned 27 years old on 13 March, and my age was never more evident than in comparison with the crew of *Lady Be Good*.

What attracted me to this bunch was Guy Shelley, who when on the ground wore a railroad engineer's striped hat. That hat stopped me at their table as I entered the mess tent. I asked Guy, 'When's the next train for Pittsburgh?'. Guy's answer was a broad grin, but Sergeant Moore sitting next to him said, 'Which Pittsburgh?' I showed him my fatigue hat, on which I had lettered PGH, PA. Sergeant LaMotte, who barely looked 15 years old and was very small, said, 'I don't think anything stops there'. I laughed and told them to treat me with kindness as I was the oldest private in the air force abroad and had lots of power.

They laughed and I said 'good luck'.

I went to my table across from them, and as I gulped my food and downed the undrinkable coffee I could not keep my eyes off this shockingly young, green crew. My God, how young they are, I thought, and then I really felt like a grandpa. Bob LaMotte belonged home with his mom and dad. Moore, too, was by appearance no match for this game of death he was expected to play.

Outside the tent the crew was joined by their officers. This scene is engraved on my mind for one officer, Lieutenant Hays, gave me a start. Hays appeared as a small clean-shaven Father Time, quite out of place with these young lads. Perhaps Hays was an albino, or nearly one, who let his hair go to look darker. His premature greyness has helped me remember a contrast team of boys and an old-looking young man.

I watched *Lady Be Good* take off the next day with a silent prayer. Of the take-off from the terrible Soluch field I can describe only that she seemed reluctant to become airborne. She had to struggle to get off the ground. What a name, *Lady Be Good*: a silent prayer, a wish, a melody from the good old USA. How different from peppy *Bomboogie*, the sly *Strawberry Bitch*, or the crude *Pizzonya Adolph*. But the Good Lady flew too far. A few days later I erroneously carved in my cigarette case '*Lady Be Good* Missing in the Med', as we believed she went into the sea.

Hatton and his boys were eager; their attitude was 'let's get in there and get the job done'. The night before the mission, 3 April, when few knew Mission 109 would be the following day, Hatton's sergeants refused to drink at the NCO club. They all wanted to be sharp and ready for their first mission. This was especially true of Ripslinger, the engineer. Along with Sergeants LaMotte, Shelley, Moore and Adams, he made a point of seeking out veteran crews for information and advice which might help them in their first combat mission. (This seeking out of information and not drinking was also true of *Lady Be Good*'s officers at their own club that night.) Technical Sergeant Richard G. Byers, a radio operator/gunner with two missions to his credit, was one of those approached. Byers, then 25 years old, remembers Hatton's sergeants clearly. 'They wanted to do well, they wanted to come back, they wanted their crew to shine.'

4

Eye Witness

TECHNICAL Sergeant Richard Byers is now in his late seventies, but is essentially the same today in heart and outlook as he was in 1943; the years have done little to dampen his spirit and grit. Like so many of his wartime comrades from the 376th and other bomb groups who took to the air in Liberators, he is a brave man. He flew 53 bombing missions, witnessed their reality, and survived to tell the tale. (Some American airmen flew even more missions. Joseph Heller, for example, the author of *Catch-22*, flew 60 missions as a 19-year-old bombardier near the end of the war.) Byers' recollections play a vital part in piecing together something of the story of *Lady Be Good*.

Dick was born in Lastrop, Minnesota, and joined the US Army Air Corps in 1942. He attended radio school at

Walla Walla in Washington, and with no gunnery training was sent to Tucson, Arizona, where he was assigned to his squadron and then later to a Liberator bomber in Salina, Kansas. From there he went to Cairo and on to Soluch, arriving on 10 March, 1943. He had thus been in Soluch only ten days at the most when Hatton's crew arrived from America. Following a lengthy period of day-to-day suspense, he finally flew his first combat mission on Tuesday, 23 March to bomb Messina harbour in Sicily. To say that he felt somewhat ill-prepared for the mission is putting it mildly, because he still hadn't received any gunnery training. He learned to fire the 50-calibre machine gun the hard way — in combat.

'Sometimes it would get so cold standing next to the window of a bomber you'd wish you would die — at least then it would all be over,' recalls Byers. But he didn't die: he survived and earned six Group Battle Stars, two Presidential Group Citations, and six medals and ribbons. One of his Battle Stars is for flying the 'mother of all missions', Operation Tidal Wave: the low-level bombing disaster to the city of Ploesti.

Throughout his military career Byers kept a diary, which he published in 1984 under the title Attack. This extract gives his account of Mission 109:

Sunday 4 April, 1943
Really cold and damp today. Had the same old breakfast — rubber pancakes and burnt toast. Got a can of Velvet at the PX and a can of peaches that were canned in British Malaya even before the Japs took over. Laid around all morning in the tent. No electricity. Can't even listen to a radio. I strolled over for lunch and was informed a mission was going off at 1.30 p.m. Have already missed a radio briefing held at 11.30 a.m. Ate a quick lunch and rushed over to the radio tent and got what information I felt was needed for the encounter. Rushed back to the tent and got the flying clothes together — parachute, oxygen mask, etc. We are leaving in a few minutes for Naples, Italy — harbor installations. We're assigned *Lorraine*

again, number 1-1591. This will be her 20th mission. She badly needs a going-over — is in terrible shape. We had her to Palermo and Messina . . .

I don't know quite how to finish this — so much happened on the way to the target. Eight ships of a flight of 25 turned back because of engine trouble and returned to base. You're at high altitude, using oxygen for at least six hours on the Naples run. We test-fired the guns at about 15,000 feet. The 'boot' of Italy is an interesting picture. On one side the Adriatic Sea, and on the other the Tyrrhenian Sea. The temperature was at least 50F to 65F below zero. Fisher's oxygen mask froze first. He took a walk-away bottle and went up to the flight deck to defrost the mask and returned to his hand-operated belly gun. A few seconds later, Holbrook's mask froze and we started him off to the flight deck with another walk-away bottle. He was supposed to fix his mask immediately and return to man the other waist 50-calibre. Our altitude is right at 20,000 feet. The indicator on the bottle registered 'full' but it proved to be almost empty.

He [Holbrook] collapsed in the catwalk and was hung up between the catwalk bracing with 500-pounders hanging on both sides. Called Lear, the pilot, on the intercom and advised him of the situation. Called Gekas, the bombardier, and told him if the bomb-bay doors are opened now, Holbrook will be sucked out of the ship and will be gone. Took several deep breaths of oxygen, tore off the mask and rushed out into the catwalk to get Holbrook. Dragged him back by the waist window and immediately began to revive him.

He was already unconscious. His face was the color of purple ink, and his mouth was closed so tightly on the walk-away tube I had to tear the rubber in two to get it out. By prying open his mouth, I inserted another tube from the main line but Holbrook bit on it so hard that no oxygen would flow through. Finally forced a piece of wood in his mouth to keep it open. A few seconds later his eyes opened and he started coming around. In the freezing cold, got his mask operational and got him back in fighting shape. We were about five minutes from the target. While all this was going on, Lear peeled off and dropped to 10,000 feet and we were headed home [Soluch].

Naples harbor could be seen in the distance even with darkening skies. Italy is very mountainous — roads wind in and about, making an interesting pattern from the air. A smoking volcano could be seen from one of the many islands that surround Italy. Islands are so numerous, many are not even on the map.

As we again were passing over the 'boot' of Italy, enemy searchlights were hunting us and ack-ack shells were bursting so close you could hear the explosions above the noise of the engines. Shrapnel bangs into the fuselage, and the expended pieces hitting the wings and the fuselage are like giant hailstones. It looks pretty bad for us for a while. The sweat runs off your face. You can read a newspaper at 10,000 feet from these searchlights. Then they close the big

88 mm or 90 mm ack-ack on the ship in the cross. Cloudy conditions allow us to escape their closing in on us. We would manoeuvre the ship — lose 1,000 feet — then gain 2,000 feet while turning right and left. In a matter of seconds it could all have been over. You live a lifetime in a matter of a few moments.

Holbrook and I stood by the guns as we expected nightfighters to come up and do battle. The searchlights are scanning the skies looking for us. The night-fighters never came, but you constantly search the skies until you are beyond their reach. You almost fire a few rounds at the stars. You'll swear to one another that you saw something moving out there. Everyone is plenty nervous. Personally, the sky isn't big enough when one ship can't see the other. Our superchargers stand out like four big shit-houses in the fog. Nothing we can do about that.

The weather going home was extremely rough and stormy. We still have our bombs aboard. They should have been salvoed over Italy — certainly over the Mediterranean. We finally landed with about half an hour of gas left. What if we had crash-landed? What if the ack-ack flattened one of our tires? We could have crashed. Some of the ships returning salvoed theirs. Our ship was ten hours in the air; maybe they won't even give us credit for the mission 'cause we were forced to turn back just short of the target to save Holbrook's life probably. We've plenty to thank the good Lord about. Will be thankful when it's over, win, lose or draw. You get so damn cold standing by that waist window, hour after hour. Sometimes you reach a point where you really don't care one way or the other.

Another mission is posted — ground crew told us. Am dead tired. Should be ready to take off early in the morning. Went through the debriefing. It's almost 2.00 in the morning. Am writing this by candlelight. The crew is asleep already. Had a successful trip as far as the radio goes. Almost froze my face, hands and feet. One ship was seen going down in flames over

Naples, a ship called *Lady Be Good*. Number 64 from another squadron is also reported missing. Won't have any trouble sleeping the next few hours.

The rumours were wrong. *Lady Be Good* had not gone down in flames. And the missing number 64 in fact was *Lady Be Good*. But while Dick was finishing his diary entry, *Lady Be Good*'s bombardier, John Woravka, was falling through the sky trying to untangle the shroud lines of his parachute, falling face up while fighting for his life. The rest of his crew were drifting down dangling from the end of their parachutes, thinking they would splash into the Mediterranean. And by the time Dick Byers and his candle were asleep, a bewildering adventure would end for *Lady Be Good*, but move into a new and totally unexpected phase for most of her crew.

5

Take-Off

IT has already been noted that Sergeant Ripslinger's diary entry for Saturday 3 April makes no mention of Mission 109 being the following day, so he probably didn't know it was planned. What he and his crew did know was that their first combat mission was near.

At their briefings the next morning all the flyers would learn about Mission 109: stage four of an aggressive quadruple air-strike on Naples by the 12th and 9th Air Forces. Naples at the time was the nerve-centre for sea-borne and airborne movements to resupply the still considerably active but bottled-up German and Italian forces remaining in Tunisia.

The first three stages of the attack would emanate from the 12th Air Force in Algeria's Telergma region, 50 miles south-southwest of Constantine, starting at 9.55 a.m. (local Algerian time). It was planned that 33 B-17s of the 301st Bomb Group would attack Naples' Capodichino airport; followed by 45 B-17s of the 97th Bomb Group which would strike the harbour and shipping. Then 28 B-17s of the 99th Bomb Group would deliver the third blow by attacking Naples' marshalling yards. This one-two-three punch would be delivered about four hours after take-off, between 4.00 and 4.15 p.m. local time in Naples, followed later by Mission 109's assault from Soluch. Mission 109 would start taking off at 1.30 p.m. local time, and the 25 participating Liberators would reach Naples harbour — their target — between 7.30 and 8.00 p.m. local time in Naples, just as the sun was setting.

Dick Byers had grumbled about the conditions at Soluch in his diary on Saturday 3 April:

Rumours are around and plenty of them. The general impression is that we're moving next week to Benghazi. Anything would be an improvement over this hell-hole. Benghazi has asphalt hard runways. Weather (rain) would have no effect on take-offs and landings as it does in Soluch. It's beginning to rain — very damp, penetrating cold.

And Soluch on the morning of 4 April was indeed cold and damp. Rain the previous night had turned the airfield's sand runway soft and heavy. It was less than an ideal airstrip from which to take off in a Liberator bomber heavy with gasoline, bombs and other potentially explosive cargo. But by mid-morning Soluch was a flurry of activity. The B-17s from Algiers had already taken off and were on their way to Naples. Ground crews were busy at work preparing the B-24s for battle.

By noon all briefings had been completed and the 25 flying crews from Mission 109 were at lunch. Veteran and non-veteran crews knew that soon everyone would be at risk. The meal was even more stressful than those preceding most missions, because a sandstorm had jumped out of the Sahara Desert to the south and was marching north, sweeping and blowing across Soluch airfield and on towards

Benghazi. Its air was hot. Tents were flapping, caps were flying, and men on the move or preparing Liberators were being swept, buffeted and roughly knocked about.

Bill Hatton and his crew were in their respective mess tents doing their best to appear brave men in the company of other brave men. They were still seeking last-minute advice, just as they had done the night before — when they had known they would be flying the next mission, but didn't know exactly when it would be. Now they knew. Hatton and his crew also now knew what Liberator they would fly: the one with the big squadron number 64 near her nose, and the name *Lady Be Good*.

They liked the name, because *Lady Be Good* suggested class, smart supper clubs, cocktails with olives, New York's Manhattan, Fred Astaire dressed in tux, top hat, white gloves and with tails flapping, dancing with Ginger Rogers across sparkling floors . . . *Lady Be Good* expressed exactly what every crew would ask of their ship: to be good, to do her duty, and to bring her men home safely.

Hatton and his men felt that *Lady Be Good* was a name which rose above other Liberator nicknames. It suggested breeding, lineage, aristocracy. *Lady Be Good* had panache. It wasn't a pedestrian name like Dick Byers' *Lorraine*, a tired, battle-weary ship needing body work, but which always managed to bring Dean Lear and his crew home. Hatton and his men swaggered slightly when they thought of themselves as Lady's Men.

Hatton was delighted that *Lady Be Good* was a new Liberator, just in from the States, and only assigned to 514 Squadron just seven days earlier on 27 March. And Robert Toner was happy too, because *Lady Be Good* had only 148 hours on each of her four engines, and had never seen combat before. What pleased Toner most was that he had almost five times as many hours in the air as had *Lady Be Good*. How could such a virgin not respond to his commands? In the meantime, though, the wind and the sand kept blowing, and 106 B-17s from Algeria were closing in on their Naples targets with their devastating cargo of explosives.

By 1.00 p.m. the crews of the 25 Liberators were in their ships preparing for take-off. At 1.15 p.m. engines would be started up. Mission 109 was composed of two sections, A and B, with *Lady Be Good* in section B. She would be the 21st of the 25 Liberators to take off. Twelve ships from section A would go first, three abreast at a time, followed by section B in a similar manner except for the 25th Liberator, which would take off last and alone.

The 225 young American flyers aboard the 25 Liberators waited for take-off in a state of increasing nervous tension. Naples was a particularly hostile target area, so German and Italian fighter planes were sure to be encountered, to say nothing of plentiful anti-aircraft fire. The chances were high that as many as one-third of the men would not return, but would go down in flames on board their flying crematoria. But they knew the risks and had all volunteered for flying duty.

The sandstorm was increasing in intensity behind their bombers; wind and sand were belting into the Liberators' tails and causing visibility problems. At times it was impossible for pilots and crews to see. The hatches of the Liberators were closed, and the temperature inside the bombers was over 100F. With the runway softened by rain from the night before, and the bombers heavy with fuel and explosives, each take-off would be a heart-thumping adventure. Trying not to show their fear, the men prayed silently. Diarrhoea abounded — but the Jesuit-educated Hatton had thought ahead, and was well-prepared with a supply of toilet paper in the left breast pocket of his shirt.

At 1.30 p.m. the first three Liberators rumbled along the runway and slowly lifted off the ground, leaving behind a cloud of dust to mix with the hot, blowing sand from the south. Even though it had rained the night before the problem of dust was severe. When the dust settled three more bombers followed; then three more. But the sand from the blowing wind and the sand being kicked back from the churning propellers of the bombers taking off began to clog the engines of the waiting Liberators. Their spinning propellers in turn clogged the engines of the bombers behind, causing ever-increasing delays between take-offs. There was too much wind, too much sand, too much dust, and too little visibility. In the teeth of all this turmoil created by section A sat most of section B, propellers also spinning.

By 2.00 p.m. almost all of section A was airborne, as well as three bombers from section B: squadron numbers 73, 90 and 95. Number 31 from section A took off just after them. The bombers in the air didn't hang around, but got away into the clear air fast for fear of getting the nose of another bomber up their tails. From then on the growing intervals between take-offs for the ten remaining Liberators became an endurance test.

Bill Hatton and his crew were still on the ground, waiting with the remainder of section B. From the outside, seen through blowing sand and clouds of dust, *Lady Be Good* looked huge; inside it was a different matter. Almost every inch of space was occupied with guns, ammunition belts, oxygen cylinders, radio equipment and a host of other supporting equipment. There was also the bomb-bay area, with its spooky narrow catwalk and its racks of nine 500 lb bombs. As Hatton and his crew waited, bombs were already falling on Naples. Nearly all the 106 B-17s from Algeria reached the target, dropping 3,876 20 lb bombs, 436 500 lb bombs and 416 300 lb bombs between 2.00 and 2.15 p.m. local time in Libya (the time over the target was 4.00 to 4.15 p.m.).

The crews back in Soluch waiting for their turn to take off were wearing only underwear and shoes — standard take-off procedure for desert bomber crews in blistering heat conditions. They would start in their underwear; then, as the bomber gained altitude and the air became cooler, they would begin dressing in high-altitude gear taken from a cloth zippered bag brought on board by each man. First came long underwear, then a jump-suit with electric wiring for fuselage plug-in heating, and electric wired bootees and leather gloves that connected to the jump-suit via plugs. Over the jump suit went khaki clothes in case of bail-out. Next were leather sheepskin-lined trousers, jacket and boots. Over the leather gloves the men wore canvas or leather sheepskin-lined mittens with thumb and trigger finger. Over the leather jacket was a parachute harness for a chest-pack parachute. Then came a leather sheepskin-lined helmet with goggles, and finally an oxygen mask which was held to the head by straps and used at altitudes of 10,000 feet and above.

Lady Be Good was timed by Harold Ripslinger to have taken off at 3.10 p.m., and within 20 minutes Hatton's men were busily dressing in their high-altitude clothes. The radio log and incomplete notes on Form 1A of the radio operator, Robert LaMotte, indicate take-off time to be 1450 (2.50 p.m.) local time, but the author tends to believe Ripslinger's diary entry of 3.10 p.m.: his entry was undoubtedly recorded after the fact, whereas LaMotte's time was most probably an estimated one given to him by the pilots. The exact time of take-off is not terribly significant, except for the fact that the 20 minutes difference between the LaMotte and Ripslinger entries does suggest a state of confusion and tension.

Another reason for the acceptance of Ripslinger's time is that pilots were usually under great stress, and recording exact take-off times was the least of their worries; but someone like Ripslinger, who did not have to worry about flying the aircraft, was far more likely to be aware of the correct hour at such an nail-biting time. The likelihood is that pilots tended to give their radio operators anticipated take-off times rather than actual times. Ripslinger's subsequent documentation of events in his diary is in almost total agreement with a similar diary left by Robert Toner, and this suggests that he was highly conscious of what was taking place.

At take-off the engines of every Liberator in section B were coughing because of the sand, and by 3.30 p.m. several had already turned for home. Eventually nine of the 13 bombers in section B would return to Soluch for one reason or another before reaching their target. One of the few section B Liberators to reach the general Naples' vicinity was number 20, piloted by Second Lieutenant K. P. Iverson. On board was Staff Sergeant William Goode, gunner, who noted some details of the flight in his diary:

4 April, 1943
On another mission. Was briefed and told the target was Naples. Going in at 24,000 feet. We took off at 3.00 and soon were on our way. Flew over Sicily. At 7.45 we started to make run on target. We were at 23,000 feet, then number four engine began to throw oil like it was going to shake loose. Were ordered to turn around for home. Lucky for us we did not run into any fighters returning. Were home by 11 p.m.. We were 15 minutes from target when we turned back. Sure was a long hard ride for nothing.

One of the interesting things about his entry is that it differs greatly from Lieutenant Iverson's sortie report regarding take-off time, Iverson having noted it as 2.15 p.m.. This huge difference is another case where two people on the same aircraft disagree about take-off time, and indicates the extent to which the sandstorm at Soluch affected section B.

6

Where Was *Lady Be Good*?

THE time was 7.45 p.m. in Naples. *Lady Be Good*, squadron number 64, had been in the air for four hours 35 minutes. But where was she?

The other bombers were, or had been, over Naples. B-17s from Algeria had come and gone. Naples was reeling from their visit, 91 of the 106 bombers having reached their targets and inflicted great damage amid heavy ack-ack from the ground. At Capodichino aerodrome, 25 of 50 sitting aircraft were hit and its refuelling area was ablaze. The harbour and shipping, power plants, barracks, gas plants, docks and railroads had all been bombed according to plan. By about 4.30 p.m. (Naples local time) the B-17s were on their way home.

Three hours later section A of Mission 109 arrived over Naples, where all but one of the 12 bombers in this section reached their targets and dropped their bombs between 7.35 and 7.45 p.m. local time. *Lorraine* was the odd one out: as Dick Byers recalls, five minutes from the target she turned away because Holbrook, the waist gunner, was unconscious after having trouble with his oxygen mask, and the pilot had to drop below 10,000 feet to save Holbrook's life.

By 7.45 p.m. section B Liberators numbers 73, 90 and 95 had been in the air just over four hours, and were the only ones so far from their section to reach the Naples area. Fuel lines clogged with sand had forced the others back. In gathering darkness the tail end of section A could be seen swinging away from Naples harbour after dropping their bombs, and the lead planes from section B were preparing to start their bomb run. Numbers 73, 90 and 95 were in formation behind a fourth Liberator, the exact identity of which remains unclear, and following her lead. The weather was good as the lead Liberator flew over Sorrento, 30 miles south of Naples, but she suddenly turned right, away from the target. The three Liberators behind her followed suit, but the Mission 109 sortie reports from their three pilots show their puzzlement at the sudden abandonment of the target:

Second Lieutenant L. A. Worley, Squadron 514, aircraft number 73.
4 April, 1943, 1745 GMT. 25,500 feet.
This ship followed formation to just south of Sorrento. Think it was 64 leading. At Sorrento too dark and turned back. Saw A/A to north of Naples . . . none near ship. Saw A/A over Naples.

First Lieutenant W. C. Swarner, Squadron 515, aircraft number 90.
Formation crossed coast of Italy at Cape Rizzuto. Then took up westerly heading to north of islands north of Sicily to point due north of westernmost tip of Sicily. Then at 1645 GMT formation headed north for 15 minutes, then east, hitting Italy again about 40 miles south of Naples about ten minutes after sun had set.

Crew observed heavy A/A fire from direction of Naples — seemed of usual density and appeared to be at a definite level of altitude. Weather along coast clear but 8/10 over Italy. Clear over Naples. Estimated by crew could have bombed. On striking coast formation turned south-east for home. Time of turn 1750 GMT. Altitude 25,500 feet.

First Lieutenant E. L. Gluck, Squadron 515, aircraft number 95.
1745 GMT. 25,000 feet.
On run-in leading aircraft must have missed Naples as it turned away to starboard when south of the harbour and other aircraft were obliged to follow. Flak but not at aircraft 95, Turned south and formation broke up about over Licosa. It was then too late to turn back and attack primary target, so aircraft continued south-west and reached Sicily in vicinity of Cape Orlando.

A possible answer as to why the lead ship turned away can be found in the diary of Staff Sergeant Jack Hughins,

70

engineer/ gunner on Liberator number 73 in Mission 109:

4 April, 1943
Plane number 73, *Dysentery Special.*
My fourth, and this time it was to Naples again, but we flew at 25,500 feet and it sure was cold. Their own ack-ack knocked down three of their pursuit planes and we only saw one after that. But he just came up to look us over and then he took off for home, but he didn't get into range so we didn't get to use much ammunition. But the biggest joke of the mission was that the navigator in the lead plane couldn't find the target at Naples so we dropped our bombs and came on home. Over the toe of Italy we ran into ack-ack and searchlights and had to make a turn and come in from another direction. I froze my right eyelid shut, but it's OK now and I will have to wait two more days before I get to go on a mission again . . . [Flight duration] nine hours 30 minutes. Dropped twelve 500 lb bombs.

To the mind of the author the actions and identity of the lead Liberator which turned from the target have always been something of a mystery, but it was most probably ship number 37, piloted by First Lieutenant Brian Wolley Flavelle of A section, 512 Squadron, who may have had engine trouble at the time and was eventually forced to land in Malta sometime around 9.00 p.m. Flying almost immediately ahead of Flavelle at the time was Liberator number 31, Bomboogie, also of 512 Squadron's A section, piloted by Second Lieutenant K. P. 'Guy' Iovine. Iovine bombed the target and sustained minor battle damage, then landed in Malta short of fuel at about 9.15 p.m. Whatever problem Flavelle had with his aircraft must have been considerable, because the following day his crew flew back to Soluch in Iovine's Liberator. However, the author has never been privy to a copy of Flavelle's sortie report for Mission 109.

Without doubt the lead bomber was not *Lady Be Good*. She was nowhere near Naples at the time, having taken off from Soluch at 3.10 p.m., one hour and 25 minutes after Liberators 73, 90 and 95. But many marginally-informed people, as well as some of the very airmen who flew Mission 109, believe to this day that at about 7.45 p.m. *Lady Be Good* led three other bombers in an attack on Naples, then turned away before reaching the target. A strong but unchallenged example of this honest belief is shown by Second Lieutenant William McCain, who flew Mission 109 as pilot of Liberator number 62. He took off from Soluch at 2.00 p.m. and was forced to turn for home at 7.35 p.m. just north of Sicily. In 1985 he recalled the mission:

I was the operations officer of the 514th and set up the crew list and the aircraft assignments for the missions, including the familiarization flights of the new crews. On 4 April, 1943, we scheduled six crews and aircraft from the 514th. The lead ship of the group was from the 514th and I flew right wing on the lead. The lead had to turn back and I took over as lead with *Lady Be Good* moving to my right wing. Just before target two of my gunners became unconscious due to frozen oxygen masks and we turned back. *Lady Be Good* took over the lead.

After Mission 109 rumours abounded about a Liberator seen going down in flames over Naples. When *Lady Be Good* failed to return to base it was thought it might have been her, but there was doubt because another Liberator — number 64 — was missing. For a brief period no one realized that *Lady Be Good* and 64 were one and the same, and this confusion can be seen in Dick Byers' account of the mission.

But *Lady Be Good* did not go down in flames; nor, for that matter, did any other Liberator from Mission 109's A or B sections. Every bomber was accounted for except *Lady Be Good*. So where was *Lady Be Good* at 7.45 p.m.?

7

Missing

BEFORE and during April, 1943, most missions flown by the 376th and 98th Bomb Groups under Ninth Bomber Command were day missions, with early morning take-off times and bombers home by sunset. Mission 109 was different, because the Liberators would strike Naples at dusk and return to Soluch under cover of darkness. Barring problems, the 700-mile flight from Naples to Soluch would normally take about four and a half hours.

The positive element of returning at night was the measure of protection darkness offered against attack from night-fighter planes, based at a host of Axis airfields dotted throughout Italy, Sicily, southern Greece and Crete, which frequently buzzed around on the hunt. A Liberator had been jumped in February,

1943, by a Luftwaffe Junkers 88 and shot full of holes as it landed in Soluch; prior to this, throughout the Ninth Air Force's year-long stay in North Africa no American aircraft had been bombed or attacked on its own territory by the enemy, though the threat was always there. The attack on the returning bomber was a clear warning that the Luftwaffe meant business, and that the Yankee bombers from Libya were no longer to have an easy ride on their home ground. Colonel Keith Compton, who had only been appointed commander of the 376th Bomb Group in February — the month of the Junkers attack — was particularly sensitive to the threat by the Luftwaffe, since the plane involved was a Liberator from his group.

But darkness, with all its protective cloak, was also Mission 109's handicap, at least insofar as *Lady Be Good* was concerned. Darkness threw up problems, not least the delicate matter of finding Soluch airfield, not an easy task at night, when security was in force against stalking aircraft and airfield landing lights were turned on only for brief periods. The precision required for night landings was clearly brought out in Dennis McClendon's book, The *Lady Be Good*, in an interview with Paul J. Fallon, one of section A's pilots on Mission 109:

We went over the target in formation and dropped our bombs. After the target, we flew formation for a little way south until it got dark, then we broke up and went home alone. I went down to low altitude along the Italian west coast in order to avoid night fighters as much as possible, flew by the island of Stromboli, then Sicily, and finally took up a dead reckoning course for Soluch. I remember how careful we were to keep on course, because when we got back all we had at Soluch was a very low-power light beacon and a low-power radio beacon to help us in. We got there all right and found the beacons and landed.

It was very dark, and if we had not been on course, or had not noticed the sea coast when we crossed it, we could easily have gone right on by and out over the desert without ever realizing it. The coast, of course, was blacked out and very difficult to see, especially from anything but a low altitude. And the desert looked grey, like the sea at night, so the only way you'd know the difference was if you noticed the slight, light line of breakers on the beach as you flew over. I don't want to make it sound harder than it was, because if you were exactly on course you couldn't miss. But if you were too high, and didn't turn on your radio compass while you were in range, you could get into trouble very easily.

Fallon might also have added that near Benghazi and Soluch the 376th Bomb Group could seek assistance from a British-operated radio direction finder station at Benina, which was the master airport in the Benghazi system of landing fields. This is where radio direction signals came from when a pilot used his radio compass.

The threat of air attack from Crete, and the sensitive matter of returning pilots finding Soluch airfield, would have been on the mind of Colonel Compton, the 28-year-old commander of the 376th Bomb Group. A former P40 pilot, the Colonel had not flown Mission 109 but had instead gone to Benghazi to prepare for his group's move to Berka 2 on 6 April — the rumours Dick Byers had heard about a possible move to Benghazi were correct. But by late afternoon Compton would have known that Mission 109 was flawed: that most of B section was scattered and that some of its aircraft had already returned to base. He would have known that the mission's 'group integrity' of tight formation flying for maximum gun protection from all its Liberators had fallen apart, and that his men and ships were vulnerable to attack.

By early evening, and knowing the zeal, prowess and might of the B-17s from Algeria, Compton would have felt, or perhaps even known, that they had done their job and clobbered Naples ruthlessly. He would have hoped that section A of Mission 109, his men, were now in formation poised for the final blow, albeit a reduced one. Compton would have hoped that damage to his ships and especially to his boys would be minimal, for the latter was the most dogged worry confronting a commander. And he would have wondered about the few straggling Liberators from section B.

When darkness came and the hour grew late Compton, like everyone stationed from Benghazi south to Soluch, would have been listening: listening for the sounds of Pratt & Whitney engines, for coded taps from Morse keys, for voices or other radio signals from pilots above. By about 10.00 p.m. these sounds began to come from the north, slowly closing in on the vicinity of Benghazi. Section A was starting to return, through a black, turbulent sky still shaken and bruised by the terrible sandstorm which had swept across North Africa and assaulted the tail of Mission 109.

Compton is said to have been in Benghazi's radio tower, which stands at the mouth of the harbour. He could probably hear some of the returning Liberators flying low off to the west of the city, their engines throttling back for landing in nearby Soluch. He was also probably in some way trying to keep count of the number of returning bombers. And allegedly listening in the tower with Compton was Lieutenant Harry Heins, the executive officer of Squadron 514; an officer maybe by the name of Captain John; someone named Art Cox, who may have been a major; and a British liaison officer whose name is unknown.

At 11.15 p.m. another Liberator was heard near Benghazi heading south towards Soluch, where it landed at 11.30 p.m. Twenty-one of the 25 Liberators who took part in Mission 109 had made it back safely to Soluch, and weary returning flyers were being debriefed before going off to join creeping scorpions in sandy tents. The last one home was squadron number 90, piloted by First Lieutenant Swarner. Two other Liberators (numbers 95 and 37, piloted respectively by First Lieutenant Gluck and Second Lieutenant Flavelle) were also accounted for, having landed in Malta, one due to fuel shortage and the other with some sort of engine problem. But after 11.30 p.m. there was a long silence. Liberators numbers 31 and 64 were missing. And in Benghazi

Colonel Compton and his comrades still listened.

At around midnight on the night of 4 – 5 April the engines of a single aircraft were heard directly over or very near Benghazi. Not long after, the engines of a single aircraft were heard in the vicinity of Soluch airfield 30 miles away. It was flying south on a journey over the desert, and the weather was turbulent. Second Lieutenant McCain, pilot of Liberator number 62, remembered the incident:

> Later, back at base after we had returned, we heard a plane passing nearby and fired flares to attract their attention. We believe that it was *Lady Be Good*. I also recall a search mission.

There was talk on 5 April around Benghazi, Benina and Soluch airfields about alleged radio voice-calls and other transmissions from a Liberator in distress the night before. Perhaps then, and most certainly since then in the years up to the present day, there has been talk of an alleged heated exchange in the

Benghazi radio tower involving three officers — two of them American, one of them British. The issue at hand was the aircraft overhead. This exchange supposedly spilled over from the night of 4 April to the morning of 5 April, the morning altercation being between one of the same two American officers as before and the British officer, and said to be in the command headquarters of the British Department in Benghazi. The issue was still the aircraft, and in particular the cost of sending out a rescue plane to find it. Still unresolved, the dispute allegedly continued shortly thereafter, this time between the two American officers on their own at a nearby location.

On the morning of 5 April news arrived that the missing Liberator number 31, piloted by Second Lieutenant Iovine, had run short of fuel but had landed safely in Malta the night before. Only *Lady Be Good*, number 64, remained unaccounted for.

8

Probable Truth

THIS chapter aims to explain where *Lady Be Good* was from the moment she took off. It differs sharply from other opinions as to her whereabouts, particularly around sunset, but it is an honest attempt. Some 50 years after the event the task of pinpointing the Liberator's exact position over an 11-hour period is very difficult, and can only be done by referring to documents that give indications as to what was happening at a certain time of day.

It should be borne in mind that *Lady Be Good* took off about one hour and 25 minutes after Liberators 73, 90 and 95; also that Mission 109 was plagued with problems and confusion from the outset. The overview map shown in this chapter attempts to put the mission into perspective by focusing on the whereabouts, activities and movements of *Lady Be Good* as well as Liberators numbers 73, 90 and 95.

Lady Be Good started out on Mission 109 with two other bombers, at whose tail she lay for navigational guidance. Bill Hatton had to play follow the leader; it was common practice for bombers with the most experienced navigators to take the lead, with others following in order of navigational know-how. Ships whose navigators had no combat experience would tend to go last, which is probably why *Lady Be Good* was the 21st of 25 Liberators to take off. The engines of the two lead Liberators were grumbling and rough with the after-effects of the sandstorm at Soluch. This storm's insistent violent behaviour was pushing the three Liberators north and to the right, eastwards, away from their intended north-west course of 330. Instead of crossing the Libyan coast at Benghazi, the leading bombers crossed the coast 30 miles to the north-east near El Marj on a heading of 360°, but a course correction to 330° was made at that point to rectify the eastward drift.

While Hatton was shadowing the two

other Liberators navigation posed no problem. But shortly after the course correction, at about 4.25 p.m., sand-clogged fuel lines obliged the two leading bombers to turn back home, leaving *Lady Be Good* alone to fend for herself on her maiden combat flight. This twist in events suddenly put terrific pressures on the insecure shoulders of navigator Dp Hays. And once past the coast, over the Mediterranean and away from the sandstorm, a related problem confronted the solitary *Lady Be Good* — strong northwesterly winds developing from the direction of Italy. Hays had set a 330° course — but was he aware of the increasing wind which was now leaning on his Liberator from the west? Did he notice that the wind changed direction, blowing from the northwest and then from the north as *Lady Be Good* proceeded towards Naples? Whether Hays or any of his crew were fully aware of these changing conditions is unclear.

Taking the time and related data directly from Hays' navigator's log, at 5.50 p.m. *Lady Be Good* was flying north over the Ionian Sea, moving in and out of broken cloud at 10,000 feet and climbing. A course correction had just been made to a compass heading of 342°. The Liberator's position was 36° 44′ N, 18° 45′ E, 180 miles south-east of Italy's toe, 160 miles west-southwest of southern Greece and 290 miles west of Crete. On a straight line from this position, she was almost 380 miles from Naples. She was too far to the east, closer to Greece than Italy.

In ground terms the bomber had been moving slowly, a condition common to all ships flying Mission 109: by 5.50 p.m. she had been in the air two hours 40 minutes but had travelled a land distance of only around 380 miles. She had covered this distance flying not too high over the sea, at a ground speed of some 140 mph, but in that time she should have travelled many more miles. *Lady Be Good*'s engines were all behaving well, however, and the delay was due more to adverse weather conditions than any fault in the plane.

Unforeseen circumstances had plunged *Lady Be Good* into a situation where she

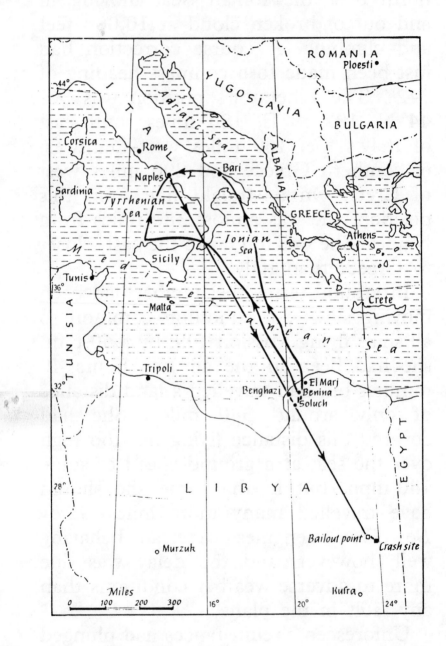

was not following the standard route to Naples, a well-thought-out route going north-west from Soluch on 330°, west across Italy's toe along Sicily's northern coast, then north to Naples avoiding the Straits of Messina. The initial drift to the east from Soluch airfield to Libya's coast had thrown them off course, so *Lady Be Good* was now not only alone but also facing navigational problems. And Hatton should have turned back. A more experienced pilot would have felt sufficiently secure to recognize the futility and dangers of going on. But Hatton wasn't, and he didn't, so on he went.

His location being what it was, and with night gathering, there was little chance he would reach Naples much before 9.00 p.m., and even less chance that in darkness he would be able to identify his target. The same applied to any secondary targets which might be reached. What Hatton hoped to accomplish by continuing is difficult to say, but his crew were behind him. Half a century after the event who can say what was truly on Hatton's mind; but his heart and character, like those of his crew, were filled with courage, determination, and the desire to carry out their mission. And this drive was bewitching, and too much for the Lady's Men to resist.

So they flew on alone that Sunday, climbing to get above the cloud tops; for more than an hour they had been flying in and out of broken cloud containing light to heavy showers. With the waist hatches open, the crew were in high-altitude gear and on oxygen. The temperature was falling, and the sky was losing light as the sun set in the west. Radio silence was in force to avoid attracting fighters.

For a brief period things appeared to be going well. Hays seemed less disoriented than before and appeared to know what he was doing; he was more in command of his reasoning powers. Hatton held *Lady Be Good*'s true course at 342°. Her true heading was 345°, her magnetic heading 347°, and her compass heading 342°, respectively compensating for the effects of wind, variations in the earth's magnetic field, and magnetic deviations in the cockpit instruments. Hays recorded the four headings in his log, feeling sure they pointed to Naples, but that the ship would cross southern Italy's coast well above her toe. On the negative side, Hays realized that the north-westerly wind was working against the Liberator and not allowing her to maintain her chosen path. They were being forced east and north of their proper course, more towards Albania and Yugoslavia than Italy. Dp Hays could see the hands on his indicators always drifting towards 360°.

Hatton and Toner were aware of the situation: all the crew knew they were in trouble, wide of the mark, and detached from Mission 109. Everyone also knew that, being only just over 100 miles west of Greece, *Lady Be Good* was well within the range of enemy pursuit planes. All eyes were scanning the skies, all gunners' fingers were on their triggers, all 50-calibre machine guns were pointed, tested and ready. With lots of chatter and cross-talk on the intercom, and lots of squeaks, grunts and rattles from the plane, the crew of *Lady Be Good* flew on in a state of controlled anxiety; on over the Ionian Sea between the sole of

Italy and the west coast of Greece.

At 6.35 p.m. Hays noted *Lady Be Good*'s position as 38° 34′ N, 18° 50′ E. Her heading had altered, but not for the better, as her true course was still around 360°. She was by then marginally closer to Italy than Greece, heading for Italy's heel; and had travelled nearly 125 miles in the last 45 minutes. With the hatches still open the crew were feeling the cold, and the threat from air attack continued. Hatton had an added distress, a problem with his left ear which had bothered him on the ground and had been checked before take-off. It had been decided he was fit to fly, but the cold wasn't helping it and he cupped the side of his leather flying cap with his left hand to warm his ear while Toner flew the plane.

At the nose and tail of the Liberator two very cold flyers shivered at their posts: bombardier John Woravka and tail gunner Sam Adams. Their fingers, feet and brains were nearly numb. Thinking was hard after being on oxygen for almost three hours; time, space and purpose became blurred. 'If a fighter attacks will my trigger finger work, will my aim be true? Does all this really matter?'

On and on flew *Lady Be Good*. Her course was no better than before, and she was still over 200 miles from Naples to her west. No one knows for sure if her crew were aware of her position, but in all probability they had to have known. And if they reached Naples, what then? What would they do there, and where would they go next? The aimless nature of the journey was beginning to sink in; the crew became bothered, testy and critical, but quietly and to themselves.

Lady Be Good's engines were behaving perfectly, with not a cough or a sneeze, nor any virus in her complicated guts. Unlike most of the sand-affected Liberators in section B, she was doing her part to reach the target.

At 7.15 p.m. the aircraft's position was probably 39° 50' N, 18° 10' E: just under Italy's heel near Cape Maria di Leuca and next to the Straits of Otranto. Her compass heading was 330°, which Hays must have thought was taking them west towards Naples. Hatton and Toner struggled against the north-westerly wind to keep *Lady Be Good* on course as she crossed Italy's heel and entered Italian airspace over the country's broadest land-mass. Naples lay to the west, but the plane was heading north-northwest towards Taranto and Bari, at the ankle of Italy's heel by the Adriatic Sea. Toner felt sure their course was wrong and had words with Hatton, but nothing was resolved.

The vigilance for enemy aircraft was if anything increased, as they really were in hostile airspace. Enemy airfields abounded along Italy's east and west coasts, yet not a single fighter plane had come near *Lady Be Good* throughout her journey. Flying marginally above 10,000 feet, the crew had been on oxygen over four hours and were beginning to feel its full effects: extreme tiredness and some disorientation. But the weather was reasonably good, more clear that not, and the plane's engines were continuing to run sweetly, much to the satisfaction of engineer Ripslinger. He was a German-American, but had no divided loyalties to interfere with his determination to complete the mission.

Catholic Robert LaMotte was huddled

over his radio, listening, shivering, and sending prayers for safety to the Pope in Rome. Before America entered the war, the baby-faced LaMotte had hardly ventured out of his home town in Michigan, much less visited Europe; yet here he was flying over Italy, laden with bombs for the land of his ancestors.

Lady Be Good flew on up the east coast, and by about 7.45 p.m. the plane's position was around 41° 20′ N, 16° 59′ E, near Bari on Italy's heel and some 160 miles east of Naples. Her crew hoped they were nearing Naples. 'But how do we know when we get there? Can't see a damned thing,' complained Vernon Moore through his intercom from his left waist-hatch gun position. Standing back to back with Moore, Guy Shelley at the right waist gun replied, 'Neither can I.' John Woravka in the nose called out, 'Nothing.' And at the tail Sam Adams added, 'Negative on my end, too.'

Forward and just below the cockpit was the Liberator's nose-well, a tight, cramped little hollow occupied by navigator Hays and bombardier Woravka. Woravka was right in the nostrils of the plane's webbed nose (only Liberator B-24Ds present this webbed-nose face), in the furthest forward and most exposed position on the aircraft, with Dp Hays just behind him. Hays sat trembling at his work-table, trying to make sense of the situation in the light shed by his little work lamp. He was dying to urinate, just like everybody else, and yearning for them to come off oxygen so he could have a cigarette. He had made no entry in his navigator's log since writing a skimpy and incomplete note at 7.00 p.m., and the whole logging system was breaking down; he would make few entries of any value from then on, except one at 8.52 p.m. But at least his head was clearer than in the early stages of the mission, when he was first left alone without another Liberator to follow. He knew how fast the ship was flying, he knew it was 8.00 p.m., and he had a fair idea that at 7.15 p.m. they had been near Italy's heel.

'Christ! We're on the wrong heading: 330° is leading us up the back of Italy's leg. Blast it! How many hours fuel have we left?' No more than five, came the answer. 'Can't be the wrong course,' said

Hatton. 'Our compass is set at 330°, so Naples must be near.' Toner disagreed: 'Try 270°, try 270°,' he urged. 'And we must lose altitude and get off oxygen; it's getting to us. When we reach Naples we should spot it, there are bound to be fires. To hell with fighter planes: if they come, they come. At least lower down we stand a chance of fixing our position. How else can we get home when everything is so mixed up?'

Hatton finally agreed, so Toner swung the Liberator to the left on to a 270° heading. Shortly afterwards he brought the plane down to slightly below 10,000 feet, still keeping high enough to avoid hitting mountains, and everyone came off oxygen. Hays was not the only crew member to reach gratefully for a cigarette. The north-westerly wind had subsided, but a strong northerly wind developed and Toner found it hard to keep on 270°. He couldn't put the Liberator on automatic pilot, as they tended to be unreliable, so Hatton helped him keep *Lady Be Good* on course.

By 8.40 p.m. they were flying at 9,000 feet in total darkness: there were no fighter planes, no searchlights, nothing. All eyes searched the darkness below. Although the ship was lower the men were still cold and suffering from the steady and ceaseless need to empty bladders. Suddenly came a cry of 'Fires, fires, fires below!' All but those at the rear of the aircraft could see them. 'Fighter planes are bound to come; everyone on alert.' But no fighters came, nor searchlights, and the only thing seen was the glowing aftermath of the earlier visits from B-17s and B-24s. Hays lit yet another cigarette, and agreed with John Woravka that the flaming city must be Naples. So what should they do now?

'Let's get out of here, but let's not screw up our course!' Toner's words were blunt, but Hays felt he knew the way: he must plot a course back to Benghazi from the point of the fires. 'Can we check with Malta to verify our position?' he asked. 'Can we reach her; can we use the radio?' No answer came from Hatton or Toner, who were in dispute over something or other. One seemed more forceful than the other, but the cockpit intercom was strangely muted and muffled their voices. Hays could see the pilots' feet on the plane's foot pedals above his head, and glanced down to Woravka in the nose. Woravka was scribbling in a notepad taken from his chest pocket: he obviously didn't want to speak on the intercom. He passed the pad to Hays.

1. What's he beeching [bitching] about?
2. What's going to happen?
3. Are we going home?'

Hays' reply is unknown, but Woravka put the notepad back in his pocket. These questions were probably written before 9.00 p.m., since the last question clearly implies that the ship was still on the outward leg of her mission, although they could have been written later.

At 8.52 p.m. word finally came from the cockpit: 'We're going home, turning on a magnetic heading of 140°, departing the area. No bombs to be dropped. Call Malta and request a location fix.' *Lady Be Good* turned south-east on to her new heading, and Hays recorded the departure time and course in his log.

LaMotte tried to contact Malta to verify that they were on the correct bearing: 320° north-west from Benghazi and just the opposite, 140° south-east, to the Benghazi vicinity. They were some 700 miles from home and had only around four hours' fuel left, so there was no room for mistakes. But they were still 350 miles north-northeast of Malta, and the crew waited anxiously to hear if LaMotte's Morse key taps would reach that far.

At 8.55 p.m., three minutes after the ship turned for home, LaMotte signalled to Malta's Luqa station: CYDX-V-KT ~. CYDX [*Lady Be Good*] -V [is to] -KT ~ [Malta]. No reply. LaMotte tried again, and this time got an answer. He responded with R [Roger], and proceeded with his message: X697 X279. Numbers preceded by X requested data: LaMotte wanted confirmation of his position and a heading from there to Benghazi. Malta's response, if any, is unknown. Four minutes passed, and at 8.59 LaMotte tried again: CYDX-V-KT ~-99 [a transmission mistake] -X279-279, asking for half the information requested before, probably his heading from Benghazi. Malta tapped back a reply confirming their 140° course, and LaMotte responded with AR [signing off].

The northerly wind was now behind them, helping to move *Lady Be Good* along quickly, and by 10.00 p.m. they had passed over the heavily fortified anti-aircraft post in the Straits of Messina at around 8,000 feet. About 70 miles to their south-southwest, Lieutenant Edwin Gluck was piloting Liberator number 95 southwards to land in nearby Malta. Some 45 minutes earlier Gluck had dropped his bombs on Sicily's Catania, and he was now low on fuel. About 200 miles southeast of *Lady Be Good* Liberators numbers 73 and 90 were heading for the Benghazi area on a bearing of 150°.

Lady Be Good's homeward journey continued safely: neither fighter planes nor searchlights appeared, and Woravka was ordered to jettison his bombs. The nine 500-pounders whistled down into the depths of the Mediterranean, there to join other wreckage of war. The air was turbulent and the plane, lighter by 4,500 lbs, bounced in and out of clouds at about 8,000 feet. With less weight and a powerful wind behind her she was travelling at more than 200 mph. At 10.05 p.m. LaMotte tried to reach a Benghazi control station on the radio to get a precise heading home: CYDX-XV9VT [control station] -R [Roger] -AR [end of transmission]. He appeared to get his bearing, but it is unknown exactly what it was or if it was followed. But the crew were relaxed: it had been a terrible journey, they were tired, drained and exhausted, they would have some explaining to do back at Soluch, but they were going home.

Ninety minutes passed uneventfully, with Hays smoking one cigarette after the other and the crew engaged in silent contemplation. The waist hatches were closed, as the novice flyers thought there was little chance of being attacked, although a more experienced crew could have told them that the conditions were perfect for prowling Junkers 88s. At 11.30 p.m. Hatton brought his ship down below 5,000 feet: he thought they must be near Benghazi, and he didn't want to miss seeing the coastline. He switched on his ADF (automatic direction finder) homing device to catch the signal from Benina. At exactly the same time Liberator number 90, which had turned back just short of Naples at 7.45 p.m., was landing at Soluch: the last Liberator home. She'd been very slow in getting back considering the strong wind from the north, perhaps because she was still laden with bombs.

Listening in the Benghazi radio tower, Colonel Compton and his companions allegedly heard the sound of an aircraft's engines just after midnight. Were they the engines of a tardy Liberator or a Junkers 88? It is highly probable that the engines were those of a B-24, since no mention to the contrary either directly or indirectly has ever been made to the author by those claiming to have heard them. The sounds of B-24 and Ju-88 engines were not even remotely similar: the B-24's engines were synchronized by her pilots and made a very smooth humming sound, while the Ju-88 and other Luftwaffe multi-engined aircraft had engines which could not be synchronized and therefore made a harang-harang-harang sound.

Lady Be Good's call sign was Faggart 64; that of Soluch airfield was Lifebuoy. It is alleged that a voice-call was heard from *Lady Be Good* in the Benghazi radio tower just after midnight on 5 April: 'Faggart 64 to Lifebuoy. Faggart 64 to Lifebuoy. My ADF has malfunctioned. Please give me a QDM.' In plain English, the pilot was saying that his direction finder was not working, and asking for a position report. The call was allegedly not responded to by the Benghazi radio tower for fear that a Junkers 88 might be lurking over Benghazi.

It is also claimed that another message, this one coded, was received by Benina radio direction finder station at 00.12 a.m. requesting a bearing to Benina, to which Benina replied giving a magnetic bearing from Benina of 330°. Assuming Hatton received this or other similar Benina bearings, his immediate action would have been to employ his ADF radio compass and fly on a heading of 150° — the opposite of 330°, since *Lady Be*

Good was flying towards Benina and not away from it. Whether Hatton and Toner reacted in this manner is unknown. Some say to this day that the aircraft was actually past Benina heading south at the time of the message, in which case the 330° bearing would lead Hatton and Toner to believe that they were still over the Mediterranean and should continue straight ahead, south towards Benina. The term used at the time for this misunderstanding was 'reading off the back of the loop'.

That night the engines of solitary aircraft were heard very near Soluch airfield. Flares were sent up, but the aircraft continued south over the desert in the direction of Kufra Oasis.

Irrespective of Hays' assumed or apparent navigational errors on the way to Naples, one thing is certain. Hays had a good idea of where he was from around 9.00 p.m. onwards, because at midnight or shortly thereafter *Lady Be Good* flew directly over or near Benghazi, then Benina, then Soluch airfield. Fifty years on hindsight strongly suggests that Hatton's inability to locate Soluch airfield on the night of 4 – 5 April, 1943, may not have been so much the fault of poor navigation by Dp Hays, but due more to a clash of personalities between two of his comrades on the ground over the identity of the aircraft overhead.

LaMotte's radio data sheet is far less easy to follow than Hays' navigator's log, not least because of the random manner in which LaMotte recorded the codes of calls attempted. But his data sheet does suggest that he made a number of calls to Malta, and almost certainly made contact with them at 8.55 p.m. and 8.59 p.m. At 10.05 p.m. he called and made contact with a Benghazi area control station, probably Benina, asking for a bearing. He said 'Roger', then asked the station to repeat its message. His log fails to indicate any other radio contact after 10.05 p.m., though it is highly probable that contact with Benina was made again at some point just after midnight. Liberator number 73, which landed at Soluch at 11.10 p.m., certainly heard a radio call from *Lady Be Good*. Second Lieutenant Dean A. Christie was on board number 73:

We heard her radio and tried to contact her. She was apparently lost and was seeking a heading. Afterwards it was determined that she flew right over Soluch and headed south.

At about 1.55 a.m. William Hatton probably made his last call: 'Faggart 64 to Lifebuoy. Faggart 64 to Lifebuoy. My direction finder is not working. Please give me a position report. I think I'm over the Mediterranean close to Benghazi. Fuel almost gone. Will have to jump soon. Please give me a QDM.'

9

The Next Day

AT 4.45 p.m. on 9 April, 1943, a confirmation copy of a telegraphic summary of Mission 109 was dispatched to General Uzal Ent, commanding officer of Ninth Bomber Command in Benghazi, by Major George W. Norton Jnr of 376th Bomb Group headquarters at Soluch airfield. It confirmed an earlier message sent to the General at 0200 GMT (4.00 a.m. local time) on 5 April. After detailing the damage done to the target, enemy anti-aircraft and fighter activity, and battle damage sustained by the planes and men of 376th Bomb Group, the report concluded:

Dust at landing field caused substantial engine trouble resulting in numerous turnbacks. Aircraft 95 Lieutenant Gluck and Aircraft 37 Lieutenant Flavelle reported at Malta. Aircraft 64 Lieutenant Hatton and Aircraft 31 Lieutenant Iovine unaccounted for.

Well before 4.00 a.m. on 5 April the 376th Bomb Group knew that Liberators numbers 95 (piloted by Gluck from B section) and 37 (Flavelle from A section) had landed at Malta. At 9.15 a.m. on 5 April word was received that the missing Liberator number 31, from section A, had also landed in Malta short of fuel. Its pilot, Iovine, returned to Soluch at 5.15 p.m. that day, bringing with him the crew from Flavelle's ship. So by 9.15 a.m. it was well known that only number 64 was genuinely missing. It was also known that the rumours of a plane going down in flames were false.

So where was *Lady Be Good*? A few people in Benghazi, and some at Soluch, had a fair idea but weren't sure. Nor, as was normal at the time, could too much attention be given to the matter of this unfortunate missing Liberator. It was war, a time of stress, when immediate military needs took priority over everything: with their minds focused on weather reports for the next target area, briefing and debriefing crews, repairing damaged aircraft, and so on, officers could not dwell on fringe issues, even though flyers' lives might hang in the balance.

But on 5 April, 1943, no combat mission was flown by 376th Bomb Group, so a few minds had the leisure to dwell on the crew of *Lady Be Good*. Dick Byers recorded the day in his diary:

Monday 5 April, 1943
The scheduled raid today was immediately cancelled because of cloud conditions over target areas, and also because many of the ships have ack-ack holes in them and need repair. Am scheduled to make a flight tomorrow with Colonel Compton, commander of the 376th. Don't know any of the details. Guess it's Cairo. Certainly hope we stay a day or two. Got three letters from home today. They are like an oasis in the desert. Just laid around and rested. The moving to Benghazi rumour is still floating around. Everyone retired early. Very cold out.

Eventually, during the morning of 5 April, the powers that be arrived at the inescapable conclusion that the mystery aircraft heard near Benghazi around midnight might just have been Hatton's missing Liberator, and a search party was organized. Lieutenant Dean Christie, who had flown Mission 109 on aircraft number 73, recalls the search:

We flew grid patterns for two or three days, and did go into Africa about 380 miles. Had we gone just a little further we may have spotted her. We also flew water grids and did not spot debris.

After perhaps a week of trying, the search for *Lady Be Good* was abandoned. Her crew were officially listed as missing in action; a year later they were officially considered missing in action and presumed dead. On that date, 5 April, 1944, the Adjutant General's Office of the War Department in Washington DC wrote to Hatton's parents:

Since your son, First Lieutenant William J. Hatton, 0-791102, Air Corps, was reported missing in action 4 April, 1943, the War Department has entertained the hope that he survived and that information would be revealed dispelling the uncertainty surrounding his absence. However, as in many cases, the conditions of warfare deny us such information. The record concerning your son shows that he was a member of the crew of a B-24D aircraft which took off from Soluch, Libya, on a high altitude bombing mission over Naples Harbor, Italy, on 4 April, 1943. His plane did not return to its base and no trace has ever been found of it or its crew members.

Full consideration has recently been given to all available information bearing on the absence of your son, including all records, reports and circumstances. These have been carefully reviewed and considered. In view of the fact that 12 months have now expired without the receipt of evidence to support a continued presumption of survival, the War Department must terminate such absence by a presumptive finding of death. Accordingly, an official finding of death has been recorded under the provisions of Public Law 490, 77th Congress, approved 7 March, 1942, as amended by Public Law 848, 77th Congress, approved 24 December, 1942.

The finding does not establish an actual or probable date of death; however, as required by law, it includes a presumptive date of death for the termination of pay and allowances, settlement of accounts and payment of death gratuities. In the case of your son this date has been set as 5 April, 1944, the day following the expiration of 12 months absence.

I regret the necessity for this message but trust that the ending of a long period of uncertainty may give at least some small measure of consolation. I hope you may find sustaining comfort in the thought that the uncertainty with which war has surrounded the absence of your son has enhanced the honor of his service to his country and of his sacrifice.

For a multitude of normal reasons, from the period immediately after *Lady Be Good*'s disappearance the only people who thought about the vanished bomber were for many years the family and friends of the crew who vanished with her. And, perhaps, a few others with special reasons to reflect.

With the exception of official military records, which by their nature must be pragmatic, the author is not aware of any mention made on a human level about the vanished bomber, other than the comment made by Dick Byers in his 4 April diary entry: 'One ship was seen going down in flames over Naples, a ship called *Lady Be Good*.' As for the vanished aircraft herself, from the day of her disappearance in April, 1943, no one was to go near her for the next 15 years until British oilmen flying over Libya's Cyrenaica region in the course of their work happened to pass her way.

From that point forward, the saga of *Lady Be Good* and her crew would slowly, though often reluctantly, begin to unfold — thanks to man's need for petroleum.

10

Oilmen Overhead

ENTER petroleum and its hunters. The story of *Lady Be Good* is known today only because of man's need for oil: oilmen engaged in searching for it spotted her while conducting aerial reconnaissance in Libya. The details of the sighting and the subsequent ground discovery of the bomber warrant explanation, without which the story of *Lady Be Good* would be incomplete — indeed, were it not for the Liberator's discovery, there would be no story to tell.

There were three sightings of *Lady Be Good* from the air, all by employees of British Petroleum (BP). The first was by accident; the other two by design, primarily in order to fix the bomber's desert position more accurately. But the credit for actually locating the Liberator on the desert floor must go entirely to three former BP oilmen who, despite the physical hardship and other risks involved, went out of their way to find *Lady Be Good*. They, as well as other BP men connected with the Liberator's story and mentioned in this book, are as much Lady's Men as the crew who flew her.

In 1958 Libya was ruled by the aged King Muhammad Idris al-Mahdi al-Senussi. Libya was then a loose federation of three different regions: Tripolitania in the north-west, Fezzan in the south-west, and Cyrenaica in the east. The three regions had been federated in 1951 under the auspices of the United Nations, but in many ways the federation had the appearance of a police state and in 1958 there were rumours of opposition to the king from within his own household. It was anticipated that upon the king's death his sons would be his natural successors. But on 1 September, 1969, the aged king was deposed in a military coup by 27-year-old Colonel Muammar al-Qaddafi, who rules to this day at the head of a five-member General Secretariat.

By 1958, 13 years after the end of the Second World War, the search for oil was becoming a top priority among industrialized nations. The huge energy needs of the war had cut deeply into world petroleum reserves: new sources of energy for the coming years were required, and a vigorous and highly competitive hunt by oil companies was under way. The leading oil-producing nations included the United States, the Soviet Union, Iran, the Gulf oil states and Venezuela.

One of the countries in which petroleum was being sought was Libya. Sixteen oil companies were exploring there in 1958, including Esso, Shell, CPTL, Bunker Hunt, Agip, Amoseas, Gulf, Mobil, Oasis and BP. Each had requested and been granted permission by the Libyan Petroleum Commission to explore for oil in designated areas, known as concessions, which ranged far and wide over a large stretch of Libya's considerable desert terrain as far south as 600 miles or more from the country's northern coast.

Supporting the oil companies in their

work were numerous roving subcontractors, who might work for Shell one week and BP the next. They included caterers, seismic specialists, riggers, geophysicists, drillers, exploration experts and so on. One such subcontractor was Silver City Airways, a company with a small fleet of aircraft in Tripoli and Benghazi. Their flying staff were an interesting handful of experienced airmen who enjoyed immensely the pioneering nature of their work in North Africa and the Middle East. Silver City's main client was Esso, but the company also worked for BP and its wholly-owned subsidiary, D'Arcy Exploration Company (Africa) Ltd, for whom Silver City would transport equipment and personnel to and from a number of D'Arcy concessions scattered throughout Libya.

These concessions were allocated numbers to distinguish one from the other. One of D'Arcy's concessions in the Cyrenaica region was number 37. Considerably south of it, but still in Cyrenaica, D'Arcy had filed application on a stretch of land about which little was known, designated Application 121.

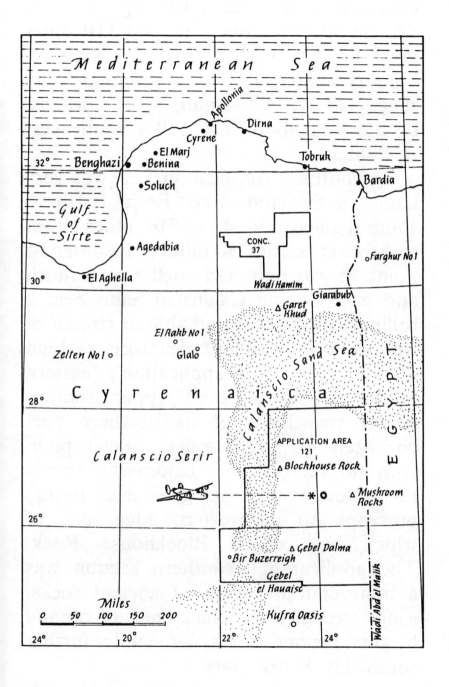

Concession 37 was relatively small in size: some 165 miles wide and 110 miles deep at its maximum, with sharp irregular borders which on a map resembled the shape of a hand-gun. Its northern border was about 150 miles south-west of Soluch.

By contrast, Application 121 was very large, in fact too large. From north to south it measured about 300 miles, from east to west some 250 miles at its broadest point. It was bounded on the east, north and west by the Calanscio Sand Sea; a rolling, constantly wind-shifted stretch of soft sand in which dunes rose as high as 600 feet. The application's eastern border was actually the Egyptian frontier. About two-thirds of its northern part consisted of a featureless gravel plain with no recognizable landmarks except for a few young (in geological terms) outcrops on its western edge, one of which was called Blockhouse Rock. The application's southern section was a mountainous region of ancient rocks, sandy stretches and chalky hills of varying heights, beyond which, some miles further south, lay Kufra Oasis.

Ronald G. MacLean, aged 33, D'Arcy Exploration's chief geologist in Libya, had an important decision to make. The Libyan Petroleum Commission felt that the total acreage of Application 121 was too large and must be reduced by 25 per cent. MacLean had to decide which portion should be given up, but the application had been based only on regional geological studies, and he had no aerial photographs of the area for making photogeological evaluations. MacLean thus decided as a first step to carry out an aerial reconnaissance of the region, which was mostly a barren stretch of unknown desert. The only maps available were rudimentary ones drawn during the Second World War by the British Long Range Desert Group.

As far as flying over this territory was concerned, MacLean knew that one could not be complacent. As a former wartime pilot he was very familiar with the problems to be encountered by flyers using dead reckoning navigation — the navigational method his aerial survey would need to employ. But MacLean did not worry unduly, because he had solid Silver City flyers to work with.

On 16 May, 1958, the amiable Captain Charles P. Hellewell, a 35-year-old Silver City pilot, flew his DC-3 Dakota from Idris airport in Tripoli to Concession 37, to rendezvous with Ronald MacLean for the aerial reconnaissance. Hellewell, also a wartime pilot, was accompanied by First Officer Tony G. Hunt, aged 34, as co-pilot/navigator, and Radio Officer Bill Colvin, aged 28. Concession 37, later to be called Rosefield, contained little more than a few tents to house visiting oilmen carrying out seismic work. Hellewell's brief was to stay the night there and the following day fly MacLean south for his aerial survey of the Kufra Mountain (Jebel Dalma) rock outcrops in Application 121's southern zone. On the way south, immediately beyond Concession 37, they were also to try and determine if a road or track could be established through the Calanscio Sand Sea to link Concession 37 and Application 121's northern strip.

The rendezvous at Concession 37 went according to plan: MacLean and his assistant, 35-year-old geologist Robert B. Holroyd, were waiting for Hellewell at the spartan outpost. 17 May was a clear day throughout southern Cyrenaica, with excellent visibility from the air. Hellewell took off and flew south-west down the western edge of the Calanscio Sand Sea, following some old Long Range Desert Group military vehicle tracks. For the next five hours he wandered over the desert on MacLean's instructions: 'Turn left, let's look at that hill. Now south . . . now east.' All the twisting and turning made dead reckoning navigation very difficult for Hunt, and towards the end of the day two other concerns began to worry Hellewell, who was not a man to take foolish chances: fuel was low, and he would have to identify Concession 37 at dusk with only a few tents below to catch the eye. Another concern was that all day Colvin had been unable to reach Benghazi on the radio for weather briefings, so getting back to Concession 37 was becoming urgent.

By early afternoon Hellewell's position was about 150 miles north of the Kufra rock outcrops which MacLean and Holroyd had been studying earlier. He was cruising at about 7,000 feet above a particularly dead-looking and featureless stretch of desert when someone in the cockpit said, 'What's that down on the left?' Everyone on board the Dakota was in the cockpit at the time (Hellewell, Hunt, Colvin, MacLean, and Holroyd); no one can remember exactly who made the comment, but it was probably Ronald MacLean.

With no fuel to spare to fly lower, Hellewell made a slow turn overhead and they could see that the object below was a US Second World War bomber, immediately identified by MacLean and Hellewell as a Liberator. The markings on her body were unmistakably American, but she was broken in two behind the wings. Even from the air the aircraft seemed to have a haunting quality, and there was something compelling about her defiantly outstretched wings. Tony Hunt, with some assistance from Ronald MacLean, estimated the bomber's dead reckoning position to be 26° 46′ N, 24° 04′ E. Then, with no time left to dilly-dally, Hellewell buzzed away from the area back to Concession 37.

As a follow-up to this sighting, on

or about 20 May, 1958, a Silver City Airways employee took the trouble to visit the duty officer at the US Wheelus Air Base outside Tripoli. He reported the sighting of the American bomber and gave details. The duty officer replied, 'Can't be one of ours — we haven't operated B-24s since 1947.' For years after the Second World War the sighting of downed Axis and Allied aircraft in and around Libya was very common, although few if any American bombers had been seen as far south as the mystery aircraft reported by Silver City. The air base did not investigate the sighting report nor give it any importance. As far as the oilmen were concerned, the matter of the American bomber in the desert was closed; something far more fascinating had captured their attention. A ground party of oilmen exploring an area 200 miles south-east of Kufra on the borders of Egypt, Libya and Sudan had discovered ancient cave drawings in the mountains of Jebel Uweinat, and everyone's attention was focused on this.

On 14 June, 1958, Captain Hellewell, First Officer Ken W. Honey, aged 29, and

Radio Officer Colvin were contracted by D'Arcy Exploration to fly to Kufra Oasis with food and equipment for a small aerial survey party. Hellewell was then to ferry the party on another air survey of the Kufra district the following day. On landing in Kufra, the Dakota was met by a gathering of children, there to stare at the white infidels from beyond and the frightening ice they carried to keep food and drink cool. They had never seen such a thing before. (The search for oil quickly started introducing some of the outside world's more modest trappings to remote southern Libya, however: within 18 months the children were meeting Hellewell and his iron bird during subsequent trips riding bicycles and carrying radios.)

Once the initial flurry of excitement among Kufra's children had eased, Hellewell was surprised and happy to see an old friend, 29-year-old Don Sheridan, who was to be the D'Arcy geologist in charge of the aerial survey. Hellewell and Sheridan had flown together in the mid-1950s ferrying drilling supplies from Qatar to Jebel Fahud, the first oil well to be drilled in Oman. Donald Joseph Richard Sheridan was an original. Although not very tall, what he lacked in height he more than made up for with energy and crafty inventiveness. Few problems seemed beyond his ability to solve. He was the Yorkshire-born son of Irish parents, and came from a large, active family of long-lived go-getters; his mother lived to the age of 103.

The Silver City crew and the survey men spent the night in the Kufra airfield hangar, where Sheridan and a few other jokers made Hellewell feel most uncomfortable with stories of Libyan scorpions that creep in the night: Hellewell later decided to sleep in his Dakota for safety. But Sheridan was immensely interested in Hellewell's tale of the crashed American bomber in the desert and felt he would like to find it. Hellewell gave him the aircraft's dead reckoning position, in return for a souvenir from the plane if and when Sheridan ever reached it. There was some apprehension about this possible future encounter, however, as it seemed more than likely that the bomber would contain bodies and other nameless horrors.

During their aerial survey on the following day, 15 June, the party got a much better look at the ghostly desert bomber. It was evident that the aircraft was not badly damaged despite being broken in two, and the consensus of opinion was that there must have been survivors. Long skid marks running along the desert floor suggested a relatively gentle descent to earth. Navigator Ken Honey estimated the plane's position to be 26° 42′ N, 24° 02′ E, and also took what was probably the first-ever photograph of the lost *Lady Be Good*. Prior to this the only two known photographs of the bomber, both partial, had been taken at Topeka, Kansas, in February, 1943, and shortly thereafter in either Trinidad or Brazil during March as the then nameless Liberator was being ferried from Kansas to Libya.

On returning to his base in Idris, Honey reported the second sighting of the bomber, this time to the RAF. Like the Americans at Wheelus Air Base before them, the RAF were not interested, saying that the desert was full of lost aircraft. In general terms this was true; but not as far as American bombers were concerned, especially a bomber whose location was so far removed from any area of heavy American bombing during the war. Nevertheless, the RAF did not even want the Liberator's position.

Following the 15 June aerial survey of the Kufra area, Ronald MacLean decided to make a ground reconnaissance of Application 121's southern region to inspect the zone he proposed D'Arcy Exploration should surrender back to the Libyan Petroleum Commission. This reconnaissance took place near the end of June and included MacLean, Sheridan and Richard M. 'Slinger' Woods, the ground party's surveyor. At this point MacLean had decided that he would place the inventive and experienced Don Sheridan in charge of subsequent geological surveys in Application 121. The ground party did not go near the Liberator's dead reckoning position, but had to abandon the survey in its early stages after a heatwave crippled Sheridan's Bedford truck. This vehicle, indeed, seemed fated: shortly afterwards an old Second World War land-mine blew its front wheel off just outside Kufra Oasis minutes after Sheridan and Woods set off to return to Tripoli.

In September Don Sheridan brought a full ground survey party to Kufra Oasis, which would be supplied by Silver City Airways every six weeks while Sheridan used it as a base. Included in Sheridan's party was the geologist, Dr A. John Martin. As before, the Silver City flights would originate in Tripoli, refuel at D'Arcy camps in southern Fezzan, and fly directly from Kufra to Benghazi after refuelling. During some of these supply flights Silver City would also ferry D'Arcy field personnel due a week's break from their rough, remote existence in the field.

One such flight from Kufra to Benghazi took place on 7 February, 1959, piloted by a Captain McMurchy with Honey as navigator and Colvin on the radio. With two dead reckoning positions for the curious bomber on hand, Sheridan and Honey had a word with McMurchy. He altered course according to their request, and there again was the Liberator. By now Sheridan had seen the haunting desert bomber twice, as had Ken Honey and the absent Charles Hellewell; Bill Colvin had seen her three times.

As they flew away, and the broken aircraft became smaller and smaller as she slipped out of sight, the crew and passengers on board McMurchy's Dakota were privately turning thoughts over in their minds. Who was this bomber? Where had she been before she crashed? What was her story? What happened to her crew? Were any still inside? Did any survive the crash? Don Sheridan quietly made up his mind that one day soon he and the bomber would meet face to face: one way or the other he would find her. And as he watched the last tip of the Liberator disappear, he could not help but equate the fallen trojan with HMS *Kelly*, sunk off the coast of Crete in 1941 with his brother, 27-year-old Surgeon-Lieutenant Vincent J. R. Sheridan, on board.

Even with *Lady Be Good* totally out of sight, Sheridan stayed at one of the Dakota's windows looking down at the slowly passing desert beneath him. He would soon be down there with his colleagues, mapping the area and doing the geological work for which he had studied at Trinity College Dublin. And Sheridan was grateful that he did not need to parachute down into this dead land: he had jumped many times before as an 18-year-old serving with the British Parachute Regiment in Germany, and knew the fears. But as he thought these thoughts, he was not aware that on a night 16 years earlier the crew of the mystery bomber had leaped from her shelter into a frightening pool of darkness.

11

Dead Reckoning

BY February, 1959, *Lady Be Good* had lain untouched on her gravel resting place between latitudes 26° 30′ N and 27° 00′ N for nearly 16 years. The fickle hand of Lady Luck had placed the B-24 some 440 miles south-east of Benghazi and just under 180 miles north-northeast of Kufra Oasis. Her isolated location had given no one occasion to go anywhere near her: who would venture into such an uninviting wilderness without good reason? Except for the reported sightings of the bomber given to the American and British air forces, the existence of the mystery Liberator was at that time virtually a secret. And since neither air force had shown any interest in the aircraft, the downed bomber was fair game for anyone to find.

The primary force behind her eventual

tracking-down on the desert floor came from Don Sheridan. The opportune challenge away from the eyes of bosses appealed to him, but he had to be discreet about his intentions because D'Arcy Exploration was not paying him to locate Second World War relics. His employers would not have been happy to learn that he planned to deviate from his brief and spend valuable time, fuel and water searching for an ancient aircraft, and an American one to boot. Time was precious: 121's annual application licence was due to expire at the end of May, by which time D'Arcy must decide which portion of the territory to surrender to the Libyan Petroleum Commission. But given that MacLean, Sheridan's immediate boss, had been among the first to spot the ship from the air, a tacit measure of MacLean's approval to search for the bomber was no doubt given or presumed by Sheridan, so long as time spent on the search was reasonable and in an area of the desert where survey work was to be done.

Sheridan, although discreet about his intentions, needed cooperative and willing colleagues with whom to carry out his special little project in the desert. He got them, in the form of John Martin, the geologist who had already seen the Liberator from the air, and F. Gordon Bowerman, an experienced surveyor who, by triangulating certain stars and other devices, could fix one's location accurately to within a stone's throw of one's true geographical position. Bowerman was added to the survey team because maps were to be made of the desert; together with Sheridan and Martin, both experienced geologists with well-honed senses of direction, the threesome made a good team despite being quite different from one another in temperament and outlook.

Sheridan was the stalking tiger type: always on the move, always thinking, always on the brink of an inventive problem-solving idea. He was casual, but not so casual as to lose respect for the desert and what it could do to you. A free spirit with a well-defined sense of purpose, the Jesuit-educated Sheridan was nonetheless both guarded in manner and hard-working.

At 26, John Martin was the youngest of Sheridan's survey team, and the rugged-looking oilman would be its intellectual anchor. He had a doctorate in geology and had arrived in Libya the previous year, often working on the same D'Arcy projects as Sheridan, with whom he quickly became friends. Martin was unassuming, quiet, pragmatic, sensible and organized; not a person to act on a sudden impulse, he was the perfect counter-weight to Don Sheridan's creative flair.

Liberator bombers were nothing new to Martin: as a boy in Norfolk in England, he had watched scores of them roaring overhead on their way to or returning from missions over Europe during the war. At that time East Anglia boasted the greatest concentration of American airfields anywhere in Britain, with more than 20 in the general vicinity of Martin's home. A favourite pastime was identifying the bomb groups of American planes by the markings on their bodies. Indeed, when Martin first saw *Lady Be Good* during the 7 February ferry flight to Benghazi, he had thought it strange to be looking down on a Liberator rather than up at her belly.

For Sheridan it was especially opportune to have Martin on his team because Martin already knew about the Liberator sitting in the desert. And when Martin learned that he was part of the Sheridan survey team with its secret little side mission, his eyes lit up. He had a sailing boat which needed a good compass: a Liberator's compass would do very nicely.

The third member of the team, 27-year-old Gordon Bowerman, had worked for BP in Tanganyika between 1955 and 1958 before joining D'Arcy in Libya in 1958. His wife and two young daughters accompanied him to Libya, and he had met Sheridan and Martin for the first time at a D'Arcy social gathering in Tripoli. Bowerman was a handsome and likeable man who, inspired by his family, had given his life to Christ as his Saviour in 1944 at the age of 13. He was effervescent, sincere, deeply religious, and precise in all his words and actions. When he learned of the Liberator in the desert his commitment to help find her was enthusiastic and second to none.

However, Bowerman knew nothing about the Liberator's existence prior to the party's departure for Application 121 from Kufra Oasis. Before this, Sheridan and Martin kept the project a secret to prevent the news leaking out to the Kufra police chief, Captain Mohammed Senussi, who was something of a hawk and would descend on anything from which he felt a profit could be turned.

The planned survey of Application 121 excited the team, yet also daunted them: the total area they would have to cover, from Kufra to the northern lobe of the application, easily surpassed the size of Ireland. From north to south the application measured close to 300 miles, from west to east at least 250 miles in its southern portion and about 125 miles in the north. Sheridan and Martin would have the specific task of constructing a geological map of the terrain and identifying the location of rock samples gathered along the way. Many of these samples would be fossil-bearing, from which their age could be determined. The geological occurrences and characteristics of the rocks would also later be analysed for indications as to whether they came from areas of likely oil reserves, and this analysis would give Ronald MacLean a clear indication as to what portion of Application 121 should be returned to the Libyan Petroleum Commission. Bowerman, in addition to establishing the party's position most nights by way of star-fixes, would tie in existing aerial photographs of the region with the actual locations visited to help construct Sheridan and Martin's geological map.

The ground survey was a serious matter, not to be undertaken lightly. Much of Application 121's northern territory was unknown. Although it was highly unlikely that unexploded land-mines from the Second World War existed north of Kufra Oasis, it was not certain — as Sheridan had already discovered when the wheel was blown off his Bedford the previous June. The French-Algerian war was bubbling at the time and clandestine gun-runners from Egypt were known to travel west across Libya heading for Algeria at night in vehicles heavy with weapons. Their route was said to be north of Application 121 but, as in the case of land-mines, it was unwise to be too complacent. Bowerman had already experienced a near-miss with gun-runners while working in southern Fezzan, when the desert sky near his camp was aglow at night for more than an hour from the lights of their vehicles. The gun-runners had a violent reputation, and were best avoided day or night.

Other than aerial reconnaissance photographs of parts of the region and the aborted ground survey of the previous June by MacLean, Sheridan and Woods, little was known about Application 121, especially its vast northern territory. The team had to rely on native local knowledge of the area, plus the general observations of Silver City flyers. For guidance they had only a rather crude map of the district drawn by the Long Range Desert Group in 1942 around the time of El Alamein.

On Saturday 14 February, 1959, the three oilmen left Tripoli for Kufra on board a Silver City DC9. On their way south they stopped overnight at a D'Arcy seismic camp at which Bowerman had recently been working, and the following day, 15 February, flew on to Kufra Oasis. There was much to do prior to their desert departure, arranging transportation, food, water, fuel, shelter, medications, and all the work equipment required. And they could not simply set off into the desert on their own; they needed reliable Libyans to act as drivers (Europeans were forbidden to drive in Libya), cook and mechanic.

This help came in the form of Sayid bin Ramadan, Ali Shariff and Abdul Gealil, all in their mid-twenties and no strangers to the oil business. Sayid and Ali, driver and cook respectively, had known and worked with Sheridan since his arrival in Libya in 1957, having been part of Sheridan's team on the Castel Benito 1 well, the first to be drilled by D'Arcy Exploration in Libya. Both were reasonably religious Muslims: indeed, one of Sayid's great hopes was that one day his friend Don Sheridan would become a Muslim. (He was never granted this wish.) Ali was an unusual, urbane and sometimes over-proud man who

141

tended to dominate his compatriots. His confident and authoritarian ways sprang from having a well-known, well-travelled businessman as a father, and Ali himself wanted to study in America. (In due course Ali's wish was granted, only for him to lose his life in a New England road accident.) Abdul, the party's mechanic, was humble of nature and less gregarious than his two fellow-Libyans. His task would be to tend to the ground party's Land Rover, Bedford truck and Dodge Power Wagon.

On reaching Kufra Oasis the oilmen were met by their waiting helpers and preparations immediately began to gather and load their necessities. There was a delay while a damaged truck the oilmen were to drive back to Benghazi after the survey was repaired using spare parts flown from Tripoli, and it was 20 February before the expedition into Application 121 could set off. None of the men carried firearms. After the irritating delay in getting away the last thing on the minds of Sheridan and Martin was the desert bomber. The Libyan helpers knew nothing about the Liberator, and

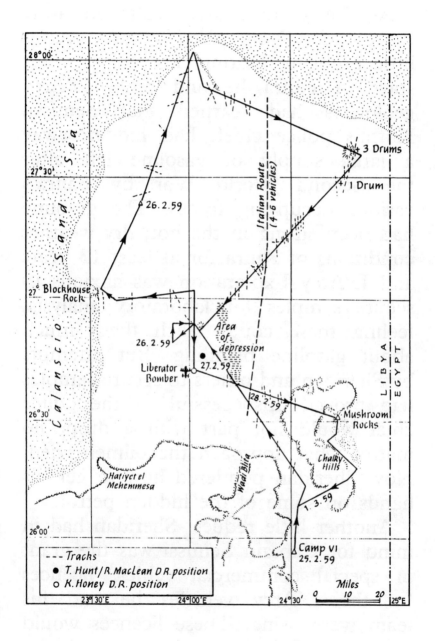

28°00'

S a n d   S e a

C a l a n s c i o

27°30'

△ 26.2.59

Italian Route (4-6 vehicles)

+ 3 Drums

+ 1 Drum

27°

Blockhouse Rock

26.2.59

Area of depression

● 27.2.59

Liberator Bomber

28.2.59

Mushroom Rocks

26°30'

Chalky Hills

Hatiyet el Mehemmesa

Wadi Blifa

1.3.59

△ Camp VI
25.2.59

26°00'

LIBYA | EGYPT

- - - Tracks
● T. Hunt/R.MacLean D.R. position
○ K. Honey D.R. position

Miles
0   10   20

23°30'E   24°00'E   24°30'   25°E

Bowerman was still in the dark.

As the ground party rumbled away from Kufra Oasis, Sheridan pondered a little problem. During this and previous stays in Kufra he and other D'Arcy geologists had learned that Senussi, Kufra's police chief, had hidden away a large supply of gasoline left after the Second World War by Kufra's various occupying forces. The gasoline had been sitting in the hot, dry weather conditions of Kufra for at least 13 years and D'Arcy Exploration was anxious to secure samples for laboratory analysis, feeling these could teach them much about gasoline blending. But attempts by Sheridan and others to secure samples had proved unsuccessful — the police chief would not part with a drop, no matter what approach the oilmen tried. Now Sheridan pondered how to get his hands on some of the hidden petrol.

Another little request Sheridan had in mind for Captain Senussi was the grant of special commercial vehicle licences for the D'Arcy vehicles he and his team were using. These licences would permit non-Libyans to drive the vehicles throughout the country without having to rely on the Libyan drivers required by law. But for the moment Sheridan and his companions had to bump their way over the desert as passengers. Despite the ban on non-Libyan drivers, however, they sometimes took the wheel when in remote areas of the country.

They made their way along a confirmed route travelling in a north-easterly direction, and even at this early stage they could see the beginnings of the raw, almost lifeless landscape lying ahead. Only the occasional desert rat, scorpion or other forms of hidden insect life found comfort there.

The explorers went about their business, stopping here and there among isolated hills, rocky ridges, flatlands, sandy stretches and ancient fossil-bearing rock outcrops of different sizes, shapes and colours. For Sheridan and Martin the surroundings represented an infinite natural laboratory displaying sample after sample of ancient earth beneath which oil might lie hidden. Each rock, stone and pebble flashed a message to the geologists. At various choice points along the way they would gather and bag samples, noting the locations in their field-books for addition to their evolving map. (Future analysis of these samples eventually suggested that the southern region of Application 121 offered little prospect of oil reserves, so in due course this region was returned to the Libyan Petroleum Commission in compliance with their earlier request.) They also found the impact crater of a meteorite, which they thought fascinating.

On the night of 20 February the party bivouacked in a hilly region about 30 miles north-east of Kufra Oasis. Bowerman took his first star-fix, Sayid, Ali and Abdul said their prayers, and everyone tucked into couscous or tuna fish hash before settling into their elevated camp-beds. All eyes checked for the dreaded scorpions: surrounding rocks had to be carefully inspected, and relieving oneself necessitated the utmost caution. The bigger the rock, the nastier the surprise could be. The night was cold and silent, with nothing between the recumbent oilmen and the stars except a crisp, clear highway of space. Around them stretched the vast, empty desert.

About 40 miles to the east lay the Egyptian border, and the team spent 21 – 22 February working along the border region. They had been instructed not to stray into Egypt: relations between Libya and Egypt were less than cordial, and the Libyan people's general discontent with their own king and adoration for Egypt's President Nasser made for an uneasy border situation between the two countries. They reached the frontier by driving through small sandy plains and dunes, low hills and stony ground until they arrived at Jebel Saada, where they saw a soft, inviting valley of sand smoothly sloping into Egypt. The geology was so exciting that the oilmen forgot themselves and inadvertently slipped over the border, but when they realized their mistake they hurried back to the safety of Libya.

The oilmen spent 23 February exploring the stony ground, soft sand and broken hills of a region some 40 miles north-west of Jebel Saada. That evening they came upon a spacious land mass of hard sand and on it, at a point some 60 miles north-east of Kufra, a perfectly preserved Second World War British Blenheim bomber with its undercarriage down. The bomber's existence was well known to Sheridan and Martin, who had first come upon the Blenheim during the Christmas-New Year period two months earlier and reported her position to the RAF, but totally new to Gordon Bowerman and the Libyans. The Blenheim had landed in the desert short of fuel in 1942 while trying to reach Kufra. Three of her four-man crew had died of thirst, one had survived. The bodies of the dead had been buried near the aircraft by the Long Range Desert Group and their graves marked with three oil-drums. Although Sheridan and Martin knew about the Blenheim's existence, her story and that of her crew remained largely a mystery to them at the time. Nevertheless, coming upon her put the three oilmen in an even more curious mood about the American bomber relatively nearby, about which Bowerman had by then been informed.

By the night of 24 February, their fifth night in the field, the party had accomplished a great deal: exploring the unknown region north-east of Kufra, gathering useful samples of its geology, and adding substantial new data to the Long Range Desert Group map. They were now roughly halfway across Application 121's north-south axis, somewhat east of the centre, and about 20 miles from the southern tip of a featureless gravel plain which sat to the north. All three oilmen were keenly aware that somewhere north-west of their camp, perhaps only 75 miles away, lay the mysterious desert bomber.

Sheridan had her two dead reckoning co-ordinates written in his field-book, and he felt sure Honey's calculation of 26° 42′ N, 24° 02′ E would cut a handsome path right to the bomber's doors. Bowerman provisionally assessed their camp's position as being 25° 56′ N, 24° 31′ E, so the Liberator had to be north and west of them, just east of a straight 323° line running from their camp to their next port of call, Blockhouse Rock, some 95 miles away. Since the team's planned movements would take them past the bomber's estimated location, the oilmen agreed that if at all possible an effort would be made the following day to locate the bomber on the way to Blockhouse Rock.

Their five days in the field had been remarkably trouble-free. The afternoon sun had been more than bearable, nothing like the blistering heat Sheridan had experienced the previous June; indeed, there had been several shivering nights of sharp frost. Their Bedford truck and Power Wagon had been mired in sand on a few occasions, but with the help of perforated steel plates plus lots of manpower the vehicles had been freed. Their only other slight difficulty had been afternoon heat shimmers while driving through the occasional flatlands. Now, however, the survey team ran into mechanical problems with the Bedford. Sheridan thought the journey north would last only a few days; since the Bedford was misbehaving, and in order to conserve fuel, the best plan would be for Abdul to stay behind, attend to the truck, and look after the equipment and supplies not needed on the short trip. The thought of being left behind in the middle of nowhere was not a happy one for Abdul, but he took it graciously in his stride as if Allah had spoken.

So, on the morning of 25 February, the main party set off in a northerly direction, travelling over ten miles of rough, stony ground and a further ten miles of sandstone before finally entering the southern tip of Application 121's featureless gravel plain and the area in which the mystery bomber was believed to be. Although the explorers thought the plane lay relatively near to the north-west, they were conscious of the fact that they only had dead reckoning positions to go by and could easily be wrong. Spotting a large object from the air was one thing, finding it on the ground was something else. The gravel plain encompassed an area of some 18,000 square miles, so there was plenty of scope for error.

On entering the plain the oilmen stopped to estimate their position. However accurate the dead reckoning positions might be, they were meaningless unless the oilmen knew where they themselves were in relation. Following various refined estimates the oilmen set off in the direction of Honey's dead reckoning position, 26° 42′ N, 24° 02′ E, taken on 15 June, 1958, and confirmed on 7 February, 1959. The Hunt/MacLean dead reckoning position, estimated on 17 May, 1958, was known not to be as accurate as Honey's.

Their next scheduled destination, Blockhouse Rock, was a small outcrop of rocks lying to the north-west. Working from their map, Sheridan and Martin drew a straight line from their estimated position to Blockhouse Rock. They were fairly certain that the bomber's two dead reckoning positions were in a zone some ten to 15 miles astride this line, about 50 or 60 miles away from their present position. So instead of heading directly for Blockhouse Rock, they set off in the general direction of the bomber's location.

Unlike the landscape already traversed the flat desert plain offered easy going for their vehicles, although there was little to interest the eye; nothing but a featureless plateau of gravel. By mid-morning Sheridan and his men had travelled 40 miles from their last estimated position over ground which was unchangingly the same. In the rough vicinity of where the bomber was thought to be they made several rest stops, during which Sheridan, Martin and Bowerman casually searched the area through binoculars. By then Sayid and Ali, who still hadn't been told about the Liberator, were beginning to get a bit suspicious: their oilmen friends were behaving out of character, and were obviously on the prowl for something in an area where nothing other than raw desert was known to exist. But the binocular searches revealed nothing out of the ordinary except an area of depression immediately to the east, and the party drove along the left of this depression for the next ten miles.

During the late afternoon Sheridan and his colleagues reached what they thought was the immediate vicinity of the Liberator. They felt certain they were poised along the eastern perimeter of the most likely of their two dead reckoning positions, and that the bomber lay somewhere within a six-mile triangle to their west. A binocular search revealed nothing. With no particular plan in mind they drove westward for a few miles into the triangle but saw nothing, so with light fading the hungry explorers abandoned the search and set up their bivouac.

That night the oilmen decided to carry out a thorough search of the six-mile triangle the following morning. They also decided to disclose their secret to Sayid and Ali, who were by then beside themselves with curiosity. Revealing the Liberator's existence to the Libyans was risky, because if the oilmen failed to find her the plane's rough whereabouts would inevitably be leaked in Kufra. Police chief Senussi, the great treasure-seeker, was then bound to claim territorial rights to anything found on Libyan soil in the name of king and country — not an unreasonable stance for him to take.

On the morning of 26 February, having corrected their position by a Bowerman astro-fix the night before, an all-out effort was made by the oilmen and their now perky helpers to locate the bomber. They drove three sweeps across the six-mile triangle, but nothing was found. Towards noon heat shimmer made the visibility too poor to continue, so the search had to be abandoned and the men pushed on westwards towards Blockhouse Rock, at the western perimeter of Application 121 in sight of the Calanscio Sand Sea. By the middle of the afternoon their work there was done and, with several hours of daylight left, the survey men headed towards the northern boundaries of the gravel plain where it joined the Calanscio Sand Sea. That evening, having driven more than 30 miles since leaving Blockhouse Rock and with some 50 miles still to go before reaching the plain's northern perimeter, Bowerman took a star-fix at their bivouac.

The men were puzzled and disappointed. The Liberator simply had to be somewhere in the immediate vicinity of the zones they had searched — but where? Could they have missed her because of the heat shimmer? It seemed doubtful that they would return to the bomber's area again: the opportunity was lost. But Sheridan and Martin still firmly believed the American bomber had to be somewhere around 20 miles south-east of Blockhouse Rock.

27 February was a punishing day, during which the men drove more than 200 miles. It began innocently enough with a 45-mile drive north towards the Calanscio Sand Sea, where the team penetrated the dunes for a short distance before returning to their entry point, surveying the immediate area and gathering samples. From there they drove ten miles south, where they stopped to repeat the process. Then, with the sand dunes in sight to their left, they followed the south-east flow of the dunes for 50 miles to a point ten miles from the Egyptian border.

Here, at 27° 37′ N, 24° 51′ E and approximately 70 miles north-east of the six-mile triangle they had searched the previous day, they once again stopped for an area survey. Directly south of them, also 70 miles away, lay the next scheduled survey area: a cluster of outcrops shaped like mushrooms which joined chalky hills of various sizes. What should they do? Head for the Mushroom Rocks, or try again for the mystery bomber? The latter option would mean driving miles out of their way and probably add a day to their work. And if they did try, they had to reach the dead reckoning area before sundown if they were to make even a superficial search: there would be no time to search the next day, as work at Mushroom Rocks was waiting. Despite the problems, they all shared Sheridan's inclination to try again for the bomber.

It was early afternoon, and they had already driven more than 100 miles since morning, but with a 70-mile drive ahead of them no time was wasted. They set off in a south-westerly direction, tired and hungry, but travelling hopefully. With treasures in mind, Ali and Sayid were also eager. About 20 miles to the south-west they began coming upon items of interest: a gasoline drum, two camel's skeletons, and a series of vehicle tracks running mostly in a north-south direction. The tracks were of Italian origin, and persisted every few miles for a distance of 40 miles until they eventually petered out. This 40-mile wide corridor of the desert had rarely been travelled by the Italian Army during the Second World

War before they were swept from the region by the Long Range Desert Group late in 1942.

By the time the party had covered the 70 miles, the sun hung over the western horizon and would soon start to slip from view. A slight wind was blowing. At a point about two miles south-east of the zone where they thought the bomber lay, Sheridan, Martin and Bowerman climbed to the top of their Power Wagon for a binocular search of the area. They scanned north-west and south-west, but there was nothing. The men then quickly drove two miles north-west to the eastern corner of the zone. They again stopped, again scanned, and again there was nothing. The sun was now visibly sinking nearer the horizon each minute. It began to seem more than likely that the dead reckoning position they had relied upon was flawed, or that they had miscalculated somewhere. They were understandably confused and extremely tired. With the last of the sun's direct light quickly fading, they knew that if they were to find the bomber they would have to do it soon, for it was unlikely they would return to this region again.

Sheridan decided to drive due south and scan the terrain to the west. The sun continued to slip away, but fortunately the air was clean and visibility was good. No dust had been raised by the wind. After five miles the weary oilmen stopped and scanned the flat landscape to the west from the top of their Power Wagon. Nothing! Half the sun had now disappeared. After another five miles another search was made from the Power Wagon — and again, nothing.

The top of the sun was about to sink below the horizon as they hurriedly drove a few more miles to a raised piece of ground. From the top of the Power Wagon they scanned the area to the west and south. Spread before them the featureless dry land looked raw and naked. Suddenly Bowerman called out, 'There!', and pointed south. Sheridan and Martin focused on the spot, and saw a rounded object reflecting the purple of the setting sun. It was not part of the natural landscape.

The explorers scrambled into their vehicles and headed for it, tingling with excitement. Sheridan and Martin led the way in their faster Land Rover, with Bowerman in the Power Wagon close behind. After a mile the object could be identified as the tail section of an aircraft, a rudder. The excited Libyans bellowed back and forth as the vehicles sped along. Little by little the aircraft grew larger. It was the Liberator bomber!

The oilmen discovered her name, *Lady Be Good*, written on both sides of the aircraft near the nose. They looked silently at one another. The tune of the same name ran through John Martin's head. Now that they had tracked her down, the men found their final steps much harder to take than all those before. Without doubt the aircraft had a ghostly quality about her. They decided not to enter the bomber until morning; there would almost certainly be human remains inside.

After taking photographs, Bowerman, Sheridan and Martin set up the astro-fix equipment and recorded their position as being 26° 42′ 45.7″ N., 24° 01′ 27″ E.

The actual location of the bomber was about a mile south of Ken Honey's reckoning and four miles south of the Hunt/MacLean estimate. 27 February, 1959, was a memorable date in the saga of *Lady Be Good*: thanks to the determination of Sheridan, Martin and Bowerman, she was finally located on the ground.

The explanation for the oilmen's inability to find the bomber on 25 – 26 February was simple enough. A mistake had been made in plotting the position of their camp on the night of 24 February, so they started their north-west journey the next day too far to the east and had driven marginally wide of the two dead reckoning positions, finishing about 13 miles north of both, at which point they carried out their triangular search. Gordon Bowerman still has his field notebook of the trip, and with creditable honesty admits, 'Unfortunately, my fix for Camp VI had an error in it at the time, and this put us off location. All my fault, and you can say that.'

The explorers bivouacked that night behind the bomber's tail. The wind had picked up, and throughout the night the men were conscious of the wind blowing through the Liberator's body making eerie sounds emanate from the aircraft. In the morning Gordon Bowerman opened his eyes and stretched in his cot. The first thing he focused on was the Liberator's tail section. Its 50 mm-calibre machine guns were pointed straight at him.

12

Uncomfortable Souvenirs

BEFORE venturing into the Liberator, Don Sheridan and his colleagues inspected the aircraft's exterior sections and the vicinity of the crash site. They had a good idea that the bomber had struck the ground while in level flight, and had then skidded a considerable distance from east to west while rotating in a clockwise direction. The B-24 had finally come to rest in a slight dip of the desert floor in a near-level position with her nose facing almost due east. The undersides of her wing-tips were unmarked, suggesting that the bomber had remained almost level during her long rotating skid. The fuselage had broken in half just behind the wing roots, and the lower surface of the left rudder was bent upwards towards the fuselage by the clockwise rotation of the skidding plane. It was this rudder which Gordon Bowerman had spotted the previous evening.

Debris from the Liberator was scattered along the skid-path from the point of impact to the bomber's resting place: a bomb-bay door, bits of cowling and tubing, a portion of a bomb-bay rack, and so on. The propellers on engines one, two and three had been feathered, indicating that their fuel tanks were empty prior to crashing. The oilmen assumed that number four engine had been running when the plane hit the ground, as it had been ripped from its mounting on impact and lay about 150 feet in front of the aircraft. They made notes of all their findings, including the number 1-24301 marked on the Liberator's rudder.

Next they climbed on the bomber's wings to look into the cockpit, and looked inside the Liberator's webbed nose from ground level. There was no evidence of human remains. No bombardier was in the nose, although the ship's menacing guns remained on guard pointing out. The survey team became fairly confident that the crew of the Liberator had not been

30.3.86

Dear Mario,

On reflection concerning your questions yesterday I think that I may have over estimated the total amount of water that we found, but having said that I am not sure by how much. To be on the safe side if we said that there was at least 4 pints in each sea-rescue kit then we would not be far out. I am sorry to change about like this but memory plays tricks with these details — however you can be assured that water was there.

Kind regards,

John.

on board when the aircraft hit the ground.

But while walking on the left wing Sheridan and Martin made several interesting discoveries. They prised open a hatch on top of the fuselage near the wing root and found two sea-survival kits, each containing at least four pints of water stored in small flat containers the shape of a paperback book. Each container had

165

a screw-on top and held over a pint of water. Virtually none of the water had evaporated during its 16 years in the fuselage hatch, which the oilmen would have found difficult to believe had they not had the evidence before their eyes. The hatch also contained an array of sea-survival gear, including life-rafts, a weather balloon, and a radio for use at sea with a box-kite to hoist its antenna.

When Sheridan and his friends finally entered the bomber they found it somewhat difficult to get into her main forward section. Ali and Sayid were especially anxious to explore the area, but safe entry could only be managed through the break in the bomber's fuselage, the front part of which was moderately clogged with sand which had blown into the aircraft over the years. The entry point leading to the tail section was much less congested. The party split up: Martin, Sheridan and Sayid going forward towards the nose, while Bowerman and Ali made their way back towards the tail.

It was a journey back in time. The mummified remains of birds which over the years had sought refuge from the desert sun lay scattered along the bomber's crushed floor, alongside decayed cigarette and sweet wrappers dropped there long ago. Other than the dead birds, and irregular ribbons of sand which had wormed their way into the Liberator from even the smallest openings, everything remained as it was after the aircraft hit the ground 16 years earlier.

There was hardly a sign of rust anywhere outside or inside the Liberator. Forward and just beyond the break in the fuselage a small-arms weapons rack had been ripped from the fuselage wall by the crash, and carbine rifles and Thompson sub-machine gun lay nearby. All the 50 mm-calibre ammunition was intact at each gun position, except for a few spent shells from practice rounds fired during the bomber's last mission. The oilmen felt certain that *Lady Be Good* had not been engaged in direct combat with the enemy on her last flight, or indeed any other flight. There were no holes or tears in her skin to indicate an attack: her only visible damage came from the crash. And the aircraft had undoubtedly landed on her own, as not one parachute was to be found on board.

Having quickly inspected the relatively small and uninteresting tail section, Bowerman and Ali joined the others up front. Ali immediately huddled down with Sayid to admire and fondle the aircraft's scattered weapons. On their way towards the cockpit through the hot and musty aircraft the party found a thermos jug just forward of the flight engineer's position, containing what smelled like coffee. Articles of clothing and other equipment lay scattered throughout the plane, each bearing the name of its owner. Gordon Bowerman made notes of the names: Lieutenant Hatton, Lieutenant Woravka, Lieutenant Hays, Master Sergeant Shea, Lieutenant Toner, and a crewman named Ripslinger. (Shea's name came from a letter lying on the floor by the waist guns, but there was no such person in Hatton's crew.)

Most of the ship's oxygen cylinders still held oxygen, and the CO_2 fire extinguishers appeared operational. In the radio operator's section the radio sending key was not pinned down, suggesting that the operator had been sending up until the point he had abandoned ship. A maintenance inspection log indicated that the bomber's squadron number was 64, and that she was part of Squadron 514, 376th Bomb Group. The last entry on the maintenance record was dated 3 April, 1943.

Other matters now captured the oilmen's interest and attention: the fascinating treasures on board the aircraft. Everywhere they looked there were yet more artefacts made long ago in the USA. Ali and Sayid were having an especially lively time: their eyes were on the rifles and machine gun, but Sheridan already had plans for these.

In the cockpit the Libyans amused themselves by moving the plane's controls in every direction. Resting on the pilot's seat was a Colt 45 revolver, which Sheridan added to the ship's arsenal for later use. It is not known if Hatton deliberately left his Colt or if he forgot it. The bomber was set on automatic pilot; the radio compass was set at 311.0 KC for homing. The cockpit also housed the ship's attractive master compass and globe compass: the former was liberated from the Liberator by John Martin; the latter found an admirer in Gordon Bowerman. Everyone was busy and having a super day. If someone liked a particular article, he did what anyone in his position would do and helped himself. And why not? Neither the Americans nor the British had shown any interest in the bomber. The oilmen themselves had tracked her down, and these wartime souvenirs were their reward.

Don Sheridan was the first to crawl through the narrow tunnel under the cockpit leading to the navigator and bombardier's nose section. Martin followed, but Bowerman passed up the opportunity as by then the temperature inside the Liberator was too much for him to endure and he went outside for a breather. The navigator's position contained a torn map, a log, a compass, pencils here and there, and other attractive things. Martin noticed that the navigator's ashtray was filled with cigarette butts, and that the closed letters on a printed sheet, such as Bs and Os, had all been filled in with a pencil by the navigator. Unusually, no navigator's log was to be found in this section.

By 10 a.m. on 28 February the heat inside the Liberator was becoming intense, so the well-rewarded explorers decided they had better move on towards Mushroom Rocks. They bade farewell to *Lady Be Good*, knowing that their work in her area was done and they would probably never return to her again. As their vehicles pulled away from the bomber the oilmen took with them parts of the Liberator's past, but it was a sad moment for everyone when *Lady Be Good* disappeared behind them. Among their souvenirs were life-rafts, radio gear, compasses, several flight bags, one bearing the name of Lieutenant William Hatton, weapons, water containers, pistol and signal flares, the navigator's satchel of books and maps, a sextant, a chronometer, escape maps and other mementoes.

It has been said that, upon not finding the crew's remains, the oilmen pondered their fate at length, but this is not true. They had no special reason at the time to think in those terms. It was obvious that the flyers had bailed out, and the explorers initially assumed that the crew had made it back to the coast. There was little reason to believe otherwise. The Liberator's remote location made it almost certain that her crew had bailed out somewhere over the desert, so the oilmen speculated mainly on how deep into the desert the flyers had been when they jumped, and how much further their Liberator had flown after the crew left her. All the evidence suggested that the crew were a long way from the coast and deep in the desert when they bailed out, but the oilmen felt certain that a rescue plane would have searched for and spotted them. In any event, all this had happened years earlier and there was nothing they could do about it.

Driving away from the bomber Sheridan and Martin had a single topic of conversation — Dp Hays. The geologists speculated about the navigator not least because all Hays' vital boxed instruments (which the explorers took), such as parallel rulers, dividers, a wind drift calculator and so on, were still in their closed boxes. A navigator working with the instruments would never have boxed them neatly when given the order to bail out, so Hays had apparently never used them, even though they were the stock tools of his trade.

Work at Mushroom Rocks took the rest of the day and was completed the following morning, 1 March, on which date the explorers headed south towards the camp at which they had left Abdul four days earlier. They had left him believing they would be away only a couple of days, so he was understandably relieved and happy to see them return. That night the sky above the camp was ablaze as everyone had a wonderful time sending off fireworks from *Lady Be Good*'s Very pistol and parachute signal flares. By 4 March the oilmen had completed their work in the area and moved on south-west to set up another camp; on 12 March, their work in the field thankfully finished, the survey team headed back to Kufra Oasis.

On returning to Kufra the Europeans immediately started preparing for their departure back to Benghazi and civilization. Everyone was eager to get away, having had enough of rock outcrops, sand, dirt, tuna fish hash and couscous. But before leaving Kufra Sheridan visited Police Chief Senussi, taking the weapons from *Lady Be Good* with him as an inducement to Senussi to release some of his Second World War gasoline and issue the special commercial vehicle licences Sheridan wanted. The inducement worked: Senussi graciously accepted the gift, and Sheridan returned with a good supply of gasoline and the licences — much to the distress of Ali and Sayid, who had particularly desired the weaponry themselves.

On 15 March the oilmen began their 600-mile road journey back to Benghazi, which they reached on 21 March. From Benghazi they flew to Tripoli, where they met up with the equipment and personal effects which had travelled from the desert by road with their Libyan helpers. They handed in the results of their work to D'Arcy, then tackled the matter of storing their souvenirs from *Lady Be Good*.

With the exception of easy-to-carry souvenirs, most items were kept in boxes in the storeroom of a Tripoli apartment building provided by D'Arcy for bachelor employees like Sheridan and Martin. (Bowerman lived with his wife and two infant daughters in a company flat away from the D'Arcy bachelor flats.) Generally speaking the existence and whereabouts of the souvenirs were known only to a few people. There was no need to inform anyone else, as the souvenirs were all personal effects for which the storeroom was provided. Finding the Liberator and acquiring some of her artefacts was one thing, but boasting about it and flashing the goods was another, and might prompt awkward questions about how much time and fuel the survey team had spent locating the bomber. There was also the little matter of the excursion into Egypt.

As for the Americans at Wheelus Air Base, neither Sheridan nor Martin felt there was much point in reporting the Liberator to them again. The whole matter was closed, even though they did feel a lingering curiosity about what had happened to the bomber's crew. Finding the Liberator had been an interesting experience, but it was time to get on with everyday living.

The nature of Bowerman's surveying role dictated that he worked mainly on field assignments with geophysicists. The chief surveyor tried to give each D'Arcy field surveyor at least one assignment with a geological survey team, but it was unusual for a surveyor to establish permanent or close links with individual geologists, who themselves almost always worked together. Being a married man, which most D'Arcy men were not, also tended to place Bowerman in a different social circle from the bachelors. And so it was that after the conclusion of his work on Application 121, Bowerman neither worked with nor saw Sheridan or Martin again.

Bowerman was a committed Christian, as was his wife Zoe, and they had many similarly committed friends in Tripoli. Through these friends Bowerman had met Lieutenant-Colonel Walter B. Kolbus, a Christian from Wheelus Air Base. On the strength of this friendship, and prior to departing for his next desert assignment, Bowerman tried without success to contact the Colonel at his home; then, unable to make direct contact, wrote to Kolbus about the Liberator bomber on 2 April, 1959. He explained how he and his friends had found the American aircraft and passed on all the known details gathered at the crash site. He listed the names of Hatton, Toner, Woravka, Hays, Shea and Ripslinger as members of the bomber's crew, and asked if any military records from the past were available which might indicate if they had survived. Bowerman's letter was written almost 16 years to the day after *Lady Be Good* and her crew took off on their first and last combat mission.

On 4 May Kolbus replied to Bowerman, saying that an investigation team from the US Army Quartermaster Mortuary System, Europe, based at Frankfurt in Germany, would soon be arriving in Libya to look into the matter of the Liberator. But Bowerman was still on assignment in the desert, so it is highly unlikely that he received the Colonel's letter until after the investigators arrived in Tripoli on 13 May. Captain Myron

F. G. Bowerman,
D'Arcy Exploration Co (A) Ltd.,
P O Box 325,
TRIPOLI.

Lt. Col. Kolbus,
U.S.A.A.F.
Wheelus Air Base,
TRIPOLI.

2-4-59

Dear Sir,

During a recent survey trip in the desert North of the Kufra Oasis my friends and I found a United States Liberator bomber that is almost complete and would appear to have crashed without any members of the crew being aboard. As the plane is so far from any operational airfield that was being used during March/April 1943 period, we would be very interested to know whether there are any records to show whether the crew were saved, or not.

From the maintenance inspection records (form 41-B) the details of the plane are: Squadron Airplane N° = 64; Organisation - 514 Sq. 376 Bomb Gp; Last entry = 3rd April 1943; A.C. Airplane N° R-1830-43; Serial N° = 24301.

Also there are a few of the crew names that were on pieces of personal and other equipment --

        Lt. HATTON
        Lt. WORAVKA
        Lt. D.P. HAYES (Computer)
        M/Sgt. SHEA.
        Lt. TONER
          RIPSLINGER

I had hoped to see you personally when I was last in TRIPOLI, but my leave was curtailed and you were not at home on the occasions that I did call.

If any information can be found we would be very interested in it, for this is the most complete plane we saw and the absence of evidence of the crew landing with it makes it very strange that a plane should be that distance from the coast.

If there is any other information you would like, I may be able to assist you, but apart from giving you the Maintenance Log (41-B) and a few of the navigators jottings, I cannot see that I have any useful information to disclose. Should you wish to contact me, please write to the address above, and I will reply as soon as possible, but owing to the post being weekly there may be a long delay. The post for me has to be in D'Arcy Office by Wednesday lunch time to be put on the aircraft.

I hope you, your wife and daughter are all very well, and have had a very happy & Blessed Easter.

Yours sincerely,

Gordon Bowerman.

Lieutenant Colonel Walter B. Kolbus
Headquarters, 17AF, Box 9
Wheelus Air Base, Tripoli, Libya
4 May 1959

tele. 6166.

F. C. Bowerman
D'Arcy Exploration Co (A) Bld.,
P. O. Box 325
Tripoli, Libya

Dear Friend:

Reference your letter of April concerning the Liberator Bomber.
I gave the information to the base and they sent it to the proper
organization. The United States Army Quartermaster Mortuary System
in Frankfurt, Germany will send an investigation team to Libya arriving
11 or 12 May.

We certainly appreciate your informing us of your findings.

We are all doing fine looking foreward to returning to the
United States on 25 May by ship making stops in Greece, Turkey,
Italy and Spain. Will be assigned to 25th Air Division, McChord
Air Force Base, Washington. Will drive cross country from New York.

Just received a letter from Doctor McCarthy. He and Pat are
both busy in Toranto.

Hope we can see you again before we leave.

Thanks again.

Yours in Christ,

Walter B. Kolbus
Walter B. Kolbus

C. Fuller was the officer in charge of the investigation, accompanied by Wesley A. Neep, an identification specialist.

A meeting was arranged between the investigators, Sheridan and Martin at the Tripoli offices of D'Arcy Exploration. The surveyors explained how a few of their company's men had first spotted the bomber during a flight over the region, and how the pilot had given the ground party an approximate position of the crash site, enabling them to find the bomber during their survey. They also prepared an overlay map of the area, gave the coordinates of the crash site, showed the route they had followed over the gravel plain, and explained how after their initial search for the aircraft they had travelled north-west of the bomber's dead reckoning position to reach Blockhouse Rock. This was an important orientation point for the American investigators.

Sheridan and Martin gave the investigators the negatives of photographs they had taken of the Liberator, which were developed and printed as eight-by-ten enlargements at the Wheelus Air Base

Pictured by the still unnamed *Lady Be Good*, the crew who flew her from Topeka, Kansas, to Slouch, Libya. *Back l-r:* S/Sgt R.S. Hoover, Pte J.E. Maleski, S/Sgt C. Marshall, S/Sgt A. Leavy, T/Sgt C.L. Valentine, T/Sgt W.S. Nelson. *Front l-r:* 2nd Lt M.B. Kesler, 2nd Lt C.H. Midgley, 2nd Lt S.D. Rose, 2nd Lt R.O. Grace. This photo taken *en route* to North Africa in either Trinidad or Brazil.

This rare photograph of the then unnamed *LBG* was taken in Topeka, Kansas, a few days before the crew flew her to Libya. The flyer is Sgt. William S. Nelson.

The crew of *Lady Be Good*: *l-r*: First Lieutenant William J. Hatton, pilot; Second Lieutenant Robert F. Toner, co-pilot; Second Lieutenant Dp Hays, navigator; Second Lieutenant John S. Woravka, bombardier; Technical Sergeant Harold S. Ripslinger, Engineer; Technical Sergeant Robert E. LaMotte, radio operator; Staff Sergeant Guy E. Shelley Jnr, gunner; Staff Sergeant Vernon L. Moore, gunner, and Staff Sergeant Samuel R. Adams, gunner.

Standing, l-r: Toner, Woravka, Hays, Hatton. *Front row:* Lamotte, Moore, Ripslinger behind Moore, Shelley, Adams. The aircraft is not *LBG*. Photograph taken in Topeka, Kansas, in early March 1943.

Standing, l-r: Hatton, Toner, Woravka, Moore, Adams. *Front:* Lamotte, Hays, Ripslinger, Shelley. (Note that in these photographs Sgt Shelley is wearing a railroad engineer's cap.)

T/Sgt Richard G. Byers, seen here in Benghazi in 1943. The author of *Attack*, he flew 53 missions, including the daylight/ nightmare raid to Ploesti.

The Silver City Airways aeroplane from which *Lady Be Good* was first sighted, then later photographed. The Dakota is seen here at Kufra Oasis.

Probably the first photograph taken of *Lady Be Good* after her disappearance. Snapped from about 3,000 feet by First Officer Ken W. Honey, 15 June, 1958.

Don Sheridan in Libya, 1958. He made up his mind to locate the mysterious bomber.

The Blenheim Bomber found by Sheridan and Martin several months before their work with Bowerman. John Martin by the ship's right wing. Oil drums mark crew graves.

The Sheridan team bivouac prior to striking out north-west towards Blockhouse Rock.

Martin, *left*, and Sheridan, stop to work on their map as the survey team head north-west.

First close-up photograph taken of *Lady Be Good* after her disappearance. Taken by Gordon Bowerman minutes after the aircraft was found. Tyre tracks are from the team's vehicles. Sheridan and Martin are lower left.

Photographs of *Lady Be Good* taken on the morning of 28 February by John Martin before the Sheridan team entered the Liberator.

laboratory. But Sheridan and Martin made no mention of the things they had taken from the bomber; by then nearly two months had passed since their return from Application 121, and the two geologists did not know what to do about the matter except to keep quiet. Their interesting souvenirs, about which they had almost forgotten, were beginning to make them feel somewhat uncomfortable. Gordon Bowerman, off in the desert working at a seismic camp, was completely unaware of the developing situation.

The investigators had also contacted the Air Force Research and Study Institute at Maxwell Air Force Base in Alabama, asking various questions about the Liberator, and received these replies:

A. Last bearing by HF/DF [high frequency direction finder] at 2212 GMT was 330 from Benina.
B. Believe number 64 along with other aircraft of section B left route shortly before reaching Naples.
C. Intense flak at target. All aircraft

at target hit by A/A. No record of damage to number 64 or reason for leaving formation.

D. No mention of crew parachuting.

E. Take-off 1130 to 1215 GMT. Believe route as follows: to coast of Italy at Cape Rizzuto; west to point north of west tip of Sicily; north for 15 minutes; 50 to Naples. Reached Naples 1735 to 1750 GMT. South-east to home base. Landed 2100 to 2230 GMT.

F. Twenty-five aircraft on mission; 14 aborts. Believe eight aircraft attacked Naples. Two aircraft landed at Malta [the Maxwell records are incomplete, as three Liberators landed at Malta].

G. Air-Sea Rescue sent out patrol on course 330 from Benina at 0800 GMT on 5 April. No report of search available.

This information, as well as the co-ordinates furnished by Martin and Sheridan, narrowed the search for *Lady Be Good*'s crew to a line running from Benghazi south on a 150° bearing leading to the crash site. It stood to reason that the crew had not bailed out near coastal Benghazi, as they would have been recovered or received aid from the general population. It was speculated that if the airmen had parachuted along the 150° course they would most probably have left markers of parachutes or stones, which might still be visible from the air. A flight over this course could discover these markers and fix the area of search more accurately.

Major Hayes, operations officer of the 56th Air Rescue Squadron at Wheelus, was interested in the Liberator and set up a flight to the crash site in a specially-equipped SC-54 from which photographs would be taken. They would cover the flight path in search of markers, verify the crash site location and determine if it offered landing possibilities. Major Hayes himself piloted the flight on 14 May, and the navigator had no difficulty in directing him to Blockhouse Rock and then on to the Liberator. At the crash site several passes were made while pictures were taken and the terrain studied. Landing near the Liberator seemed possible, so arrangements got under way to inspect the bomber on the ground without delay. But the flight over the course and wreckage area failed to show evidence of crew remains, so the location of the bail-out area remained the critical question.

The first of many visits to the crash site by the team from Frankfurt took place on 26 May and revealed many things, but gave no clues as to the whereabouts of the Lady's Men. The investigators' report to Washington describing their observations covered 21 items, two of which read:

Although the sextant, bomb-sight, master chronometer, IFF radio and small-arms were missing when the first American party investigated the bomber, it was later determined that these items had been removed by the British ground party. The small-arms included a Thompson sub-machine gun and two carbines which were reportedly turned over to the Libyan police at Kufra.

The life-rafts were still in place in the top fuselage and were removed by the Libyan personnel of the British ground party.

The comments about missing *Lady Be Good* equipment marked the beginning of worry for the men who had gone out of their way to track down the bomber, as well as causing some concern to D'Arcy Exploration. The Americans wanted the equipment taken from the bomber back, and by a variety of means eventually recovered it from the storeroom of the Tripoli bachelor flats. The incident caused embarrassment for innocent D'Arcy executives who knew nothing of the equipment, and discomfiture and anxiety for the men responsible for finding and reporting the whereabouts of *Lady Be Good*. Sightings of the bomber had been reported to the Americans the previous May and to the RAF in June by Silver City Airways; neither had shown any interest, so American zeal in recovering a few bits and pieces a year later seemed excessive. The whole affair left a decidedly sour taste in the mouths of the men who had done so much to find *Lady Be Good*, and at the end of the day they were happy to see the last of most of their uncomfortable souvenirs.

Until the last days of May, 1959, the general public throughout America or anywhere else knew nothing about the finding of *Lady Be Good*. But on Sunday 31 May an English-language newspaper in Tripoli, the *Sunday Ghibli*, published an account of the missing B-24 and listed the names of the six crew members originally reported by Bowerman in his letter to Kolbus. Before then the Frankfurt investigators had placed tight censorship on the case and permitted only a casual account to be written for the Wheelus Air Base newspaper, *Tripoli Trotter*, which made no mention of crew members on the grounds that all information concerning the crew was unavailable for publication until after the investigation was completed.

This was the policy in such cases for good and obvious reasons, and was understood by the air base personnel, but when the article listing some crew names appeared in the local press it was clear to the investigators that too much information was already in the hands of the public. US press representatives all agreed to withhold the names of the crew from their dispatches, but the hand of the investigators had been forced and the Wheelus authorities released the story during the first days of June. They suggested that *Lady Be Good* had been found 'recently', whereas she had actually been located over three months earlier on 27 February.

By now the cat was so far out of the bag that the Wheelus authorities had to release the remainder of crew names not mentioned in the *Sunday Ghibli* on 31 May: the full complement of names appeared in the same newspaper on Sunday 14 June. This story once again suggested that *Lady Be Good* had been found 'recently'. To the Libyan Petroleum Commission these newspaper stories meant that D'Arcy was operating in Application 121 after their annual application licence had expired, which caused D'Arcy considerable trouble with the Libyan authorities. D'Arcy was only

No. 597   Sunday 14th June, 1959   Price 23 Mils

Sunday Ghibli

Published every Sunday in Tripoli, Tripolitania Province of the United Kingdom of Libya

Full list of names now released

Search Is Launched For Dead Crewmen

AN intensive ground-search is now under way, under the direction of the US Army Mortuary Service, in an attempt to find the bodies of the crew of the Liberator bomber discovered recently after lying for 16 years in the Libyan desert.

It is now thought that the airmen, who have been listed as missing, believed dead since they failed to return from a daylight bombing raid on Naples in 1943, parachuted from the B-24, somewhere near the spot where it was found, nearly 400 miles from their coastal base.

The plane had a crew of nine. In addition to the six names published exclusively by the *Sunday Ghibli* recently Hatton, Hayes, Toner, Worovha, Ripslinger and Shea (now reported to Shelley) three more have been released by the USAF authorities: LaMotte, Moore and Adams.

It is thought that all nine of the crew must have perished from hunger and thirst in the open desert. In reconstructing the probable course of events, with a view to helping the US Army Service in their search, the authorities have called in ex-bomber flyers of World War II who had operational B-24 experience.

Barren Country

The search is currently quartering an area some 40 to 60 miles square, with the downed bomber as its centre. The zone is in some of the most barren desert country in Libya.

The B-24, originally discovered by a geological survey team of the BP oil company, contained clothing hanging on hooks; food, cigarettes, water and coffee in good condition; and fire extinguishers, oxygen bottles and a radio all functioning properly. During the 16 years that had passed since the plane crashed on its present site no human being had seen it.

believed when Gordon Bowerman's astro-fix observations of February were used as evidence.

Not all of *Lady Be Good*'s souvenirs were recovered by the Americans. Sheridan, Martin and Bowerman managed to retain the mementoes they really wanted: the master compass, the globe compass, Hatton's flight bag and a few navigational items such as the dead reckoning navigation satchel and a wind drift calculator with the name Dp Hays scratched on it. Bowerman gave the calculator to a colleague in Tripoli, and John Martin eventually donated his master compass to the US Air Force Museum at Wright-Patterson Air Force Base in Dayton, Ohio. Martin used Hatton's flight bag for years in his travels before giving it away. Gordon Bowerman's globe compass was stolen from his Land Rover in Tripoli, but the children's swings at his home were partly constructed from straps and snap-hooks taken from *Lady Be Good*. The weather balloon taken from the fuselage hatch above *Lady Be Good*'s left wing was released in the desert by Martin during March, 1959. One of *Lady*

Be Good's box-kites was until recently in the possession of Gordon Bowerman; the other was lost over cliffs near Sydney, Australia, by the young son of a friend to whom John Martin had given it. Don Sheridan still retains a few items from the aircraft; various other odds and ends taken from *Lady Be Good* have found honourable homes throughout Britain and beyond.

Since *Lady Be Good* was found many investigators and oilmen have visited her, and it is no exaggeration to say that souvenirs or parts of *Lady Be Good*'s body can now be found scattered in many countries across the world. An array of parts dismantled from the bomber by the RAF in 1968 were last seen by the author in Scottsdale, Arizona, in 1985. As a matter of interest, though, after years of research the author possesses nothing from *Lady Be Good* except her story.

But what about the Lady's Men? Whatever became of them?

13

Crew Search

THE thorny problem of what had become of *Lady Be Good*'s crew was given to investigators Fuller and Neep of the US Army Mortuary System to solve. They had an increasingly hot potato on their hands, which is why some of the bomber's finders were somewhat harassed. The US Air Force came under intense pressure from the American media to provide answers about the Liberator's crew. The US Army were also investigating the whereabouts of the missing flyers, because during the Second World War the air force had been part of the army.

The news early in June of *Lady Be Good*'s discovery triggered off tremendous speculation in the American press as to the fate of the lost crew, and the flyers' relatives were stubbornly asking the American military for more information about their long-lost loved ones. The mysterious circumstances of the Liberator's discovery so many years after the war, and in such a remote part of North Africa, captured the interest and imagination of the American nation. Military authorities dug deep into dusty Second World War personnel records stored in St Louis. Badgered by the press, senior officers in both army and air force knew that a major effort must be made to establish the fate of *Lady Be Good*'s crew. Only then would the American people, its news media and the relatives of the missing men be satisfied.

Hungry for news, some of the American press latched on to a bizarre rumour that travelling nomads had come upon *Lady Be Good*'s crew, captured them, and perhaps even sold them into slavery. Some went so far as to speculate that a few if not all of the crew might still be living, but these silly speculations were soon seen for the nonsense they were. The more serious press, accustomed to getting what they wanted from the Pentagon, demanded hard facts. This list of questions posed by one news feature writer after the first overnight search-party returned from the scene of the crash shows the type and extent of information requested:

1. May I have a copy or photostat of any flight logs or other such record found with the B-24?
2. Was the bomber set on automatic pilot when found?
3. Who were the squadron commander, operations officer, executive officer and intelligence officer on 4 April, 1943?
4. What were the numbers of the plane's squadron and group?
5. What was the exact date of the flight itself?
6. What was the exact take-off time of the mission?
7. Do War Department records indicate exactly when the B-24 was reported missing?
8. What time should the B-24 have landed at Soluch if it made the raid with the rest of the squadron?
9. What were the exact weather conditions at Soluch at the time the

bomber was lost?

10. How many missions had the B-24 flown prior to its last flight? Were there any markings on the fuselage to indicate that the crew had shot down any enemy planes?

11. How many missions had the crew flown?

12. Did on-the-scene searchers report any damage to the B-24 by anti-aircraft fire or machine guns? Was there any old, patched damage?

13. Was there an emergency hand-operated type radio in the B-24? If so, did it work?

14. Was the B-24's compass operable? Its radio compass?

15. Was the B-24's landing gear up or down when it was found?

As American interest in the mystery grew, with the press referring to *Lady Be Good* as the Ghost Bomber of the Desert, it became abundantly clear to the military that the high-profile story of the Liberator and her men would not subside until her crew were found. To get to the bottom of the mystery an all-out search for the

194

crew had to be made in the desert, both from the air and on the ground.

The search cost a fortune, and brought into play C-47 aircraft, helicopters, an array of supplies and equipment of all kinds, vehicles of every conceivable capability, civilians with desert expertise, large numbers of volunteers, and all of the basic requirements of shelter, food, water and so on needed by the searchers. It took the better part of six weeks to gather all the necessary equipment and civilian and military personnel. The organizational aspects of all this were staggering, and the costs embarrassingly open-ended.

By the middle of July the expedition, led by investigators Fuller and Neep, was ready to get under way. For more than three months they methodically and systematically searched a vast tract of the gravel plain north of the crash site up to and including the margins of the Calanscio Sand Sea, covering an area of 5,500 square miles; an area, one might add, five times the size of the state of Rhode Island in America, and nearly three-quarters the size of Wales. The investigators came upon a wealth of evidence which clearly showed where *Lady Be Good*'s crew had been, including many markers they had left for any rescuers who came along, and personal equipment discarded by the flyers as they struggled north-west across the gravel plain through stretches of desert etched with British and Italian military vehicle tracks.

But no remains were found of the crew themselves, and the search was finally abandoned in October, 1959. There seemed little point in continuing: no expense had been spared, and the army and air force had done all they could. The American writer Pat Frank visited the desert plain in August, 1959, to research a story published in This Week magazine on 4 October that year:

As I write this, it appears that the crew of *Lady Be Good* did get to the Sand Sea, and that the desert has taken them, and holds them, and will always hold them.

With the search over, Myron Fuller and Wesley Neep sat down to produce an exhaustive 25-page report, sent to the commanding general of the US Air Force in Washington on 17 November, 1959. The final section read:

The following are conclusions reached by investigators based upon known facts and reasonable inferences therefrom.

On the night of 3 April, 1943 [should have been 4 April], the B-24 was returning from an aborted high level mission over Naples, Italy. The aircraft flew on a 150° course towards Benina airfield. The craft radioed for a directional reading from the HF/DF station at Benina and received a reading of 330° from Benina. The actions of the pilot in flying 440 miles into the desert, however, indicate the navigator probably took a reciprocal reading off the back of the radio directional loop antenna from a position beyond and south of Benina but 'on course'. The pilot flew on into the desert, thinking he was still over the Mediterranean and on his way to Benina.

The crew, walking north, all struck Second World War vehicle trails and proceeded along them. Eight crewmen, as evidenced by markers left, found the 340° trail. One member landed midst the 20° trail and proceeded along it for an undetermined distance, and just short of its intersection with the 340° trail he turned west and walked on a compass heading of 325°.

The eight crewmen, having left markers on the 340° trail which was the direction to their base, most certainly continued along the trail into the Sand Sea. The one crewman walking overland at 325° would eventually strike trails observed curving north-east of Blockhouse Rock and into the dunes searched in areas F and G shown on the attached overlay. This member would most likely follow those trails since they would offer passage through the dunes now visible to him.

All the evidence indicates that if the crew members had died on the gravel plain their remains would be evident on the surface. The evidence further indicates that the crew walked north. In a virtually trackless wasteland, men could be expected to follow a trail heading in their direction as long as they retained control of their faculties. All of the areas along trails available to the crew in the direction of their travel were searched well into the sand dunes.

Experience of desert personnel in addition to observations of investigators indicates that remains would be covered with sand during the intervening 16 years. The only areas observed on the Sand Sea where remains would not be covered were the bared lava intrusions in the northern part of the area. [There were no bared lava intrusions in the area.]

Screening of the Sand Sea from the entrance of the 340° trail to within five miles of the northern border eliminated the possibility of Italian trucks and 10 [sic] remains being in an area in which the crew could be expected to travel.

Based upon this reasoning it is the conclusion of the investigators that the crew members perished in the sand dunes and have been covered by sands.

On 2 February, 1960, three months after the Fuller/Neep report, CBS Television, one of America's giant network stations, broadcast a documentary programme about *Lady Be Good* in its Armstrong Circle Theatre series. Given the facts then known about the story, the show tried to explain the elusiveness of the crew's remains despite the prolonged and expensive search conducted by the US Army Mortuary System. The show concluded by suggesting that the remains of the crewmen lay buried under the sands forever.

14

Jump Time

ON reaching the coast and before communicating with Benina radio at 00.12 a.m. on Monday 5 April, 1943, *Lady Be Good*'s course was close to 150°. In trying to locate Soluch airfield, she flew over or just past her base on a bearing of 150° and headed south-east over the desert at an altitude below 5,000 feet. Throughout this time Hatton was certain that he was still over the Mediterranean.

But he and his crew were perplexed and annoyed, because so many things had gone wrong for them during Mission 109. They had embarked on their first combat mission with such high hopes, wanting to excel as a crew, make their mark as brave Americans, and shine for their bomb group and the folks back home. Instead, they had failed in every respect: they had not bombed their target, they had let down their group, and they had succeeded only in getting lost. What a disgrace! To a man the crew felt discouraged, dismayed, disappointed and second-rate. Each flyer was painfully aware that they had floundered as a crew: circumstances had dominated their actions, and they had not controlled or overcome events to their satisfaction.

Urged along by a good tail-wind from the north, *Lady Be Good* flew further and further south away from Soluch at a rapid clip. Her crew did not see the flares sent up when her engines were heard over the airfield shortly after midnight, and by 12.30 a.m. she was flying through sky dotted with cloudy patches of sand particles still hanging in the air from the sandstorm which had dogged the take-off of Mission 109's B section. Clusters of these cloud-like particles hung listlessly a few thousand feet above the ground like large shapeless balloons, and made visibility difficult for Hatton. They may even have prevented any of the crew from spotting the signal flares as they flew over or near Soluch.

Through breaks in the sand clouds crew

members would catch sight of what they thought was the ocean below, but which was actually rolling sand dunes: under certain visibility conditions the two look much the same from the air. But the sight of what was taken to be the ocean, as well as the hour of night, contributed to Hatton and Toner's belief that they were still over the Mediterranean, very near Benghazi's coast; certainly not that they had crossed the coast, passed Soluch, and were flying south away from home.

Hatton was still trying to use his automatic direction finder, but the ADF's needle didn't move. He tried his radio again: 'Faggart 64 to Lifebuoy. Faggart 64 to Lifebuoy. My ADF has malfunctioned. Please give me a QDM.' Robert LaMotte was also at his radio tapping out messages, trying to reach Benina, Soluch, or anybody else who could hear him. He too was getting no reply.

By 1.00 a.m. *Lady Be Good* had been in the air for almost ten hours and fuel was running low: the cockpit's fuel gauges were reading almost empty, but such gauges were sometimes well off the mark. Toner speculated on their location.

'North is behind us, west is to our right, the ocean, we think, is below. Benina gave us our present bearing, so where in God's name can we be?' No one knew — least of all Dp Hays, who was feeling a total failure and responsible for letting everyone down throughout Mission 109. And still no one responded to their radio calls.

Approaching 2.00 a.m., engines one, two, and three were running out of fuel; only the right outboard engine had sufficient to keep going. Hatton gave the command for everyone to gather at the bomb-bay doors and prepare to jump. There was time for one last message: 'Faggart 64 to Lifebuoy. Faggart 64 to Lifebuoy. My ADF is not working. Think I'm over the Med close to Benghazi. Fuel gone. Jumping . . . ' Hatton feathered the propellers on engines one, two and three, thereby automatically shutting them down. The cumbersome Liberator continued awkwardly on her right outboard engine only, and he had to make clear-headed trim corrections to keep the aircraft from swinging left. *Lady Be Good* was now flying over the featureless desert plain which, 15 years later, would comprise the northernmost stretch of D'Arcy Exploration's Application 121.

Back in war-time Britain, young Don Sheridan, John Martin and Gordon Bowerman slept soundly in their beds. Seventeen-year-old Ronald MacLean shivered in a tent, on a camping expedition in Scotland's Grampian mountains. The youths had lived through the Battle of Britain and the constant threat of aerial bombardment, so they knew all about fighter planes and bombers, air raids and black-outs. But they knew nothing about the nine American flyers whose aircraft they would find 16 years later.

In Soluch, 25-year-old Dick Byers was inscribing his diary entry by candlelight: it was almost 2.00 a.m., and he wrote that a ship called *Lady Be Good* had been seen going down in flames over Naples. He was unaware that, far from going down in flames, *Lady Be Good* had long since flown past Soluch and was more than 400 miles to the south of where he sat, with her crew poised to jump. The time had come for the airmen to bail out; the dreaded jump time.

Lady Be Good was flying on automatic pilot, but Hatton remained in the cockpit. He had little faith in the auto-pilot, and wanted to make sure that the ship flew steady and true for his crew to bail out. The bomb-bay doors in the plane's belly were open, with the crew ready to go when Hatton gave the order. Believing they were about to jump into the Mediterranean, they were wearing Mae West life-jackets over their leather high-altitude gear under their parachute harnesses, and had discarded all clothing and equipment not thought essential. Virtually no food or water was being taken. The men shook hands and wished each other well: they had never jumped before.

With the last engine gasping for fuel Hatton gave the order to jump, then left the cockpit and quickly made his way back to the open bomb-bay doors in the belly of the Liberator. He remembered telling his sister Elizabeth the year before that he didn't like Liberators because they were difficult for a pilot to jump from. Without hesitation the men started dropping from the plane one at a time: first Woravka, then Hays, Ripslinger, Shelley, Moore, LaMotte, Adams, Toner, and finally Hatton.

Once out of the aircraft the crew counted to three before pulling their ripcords. One after another the parachutes popped open, but John Woravka was in trouble. His shroud lines were tangled around his body, and, holding his first aid kit in one hand, he was struggling to free the shroud lines with the other. Fighting for his life, he fell downwards faster than the others, on his back with his face up. 'Holy Mary, Mother of God, help me!'

Hatton, Toner, Hays, Ripslinger, LaMotte, Shelley, Adams and Moore floated downwards, dangling on the ends of their parachutes, thinking that their next struggle would be with the ocean below. Suddenly they saw what they thought was land, and braced themselves to hit the ground. They were in the desert, not the Mediterranean. Bruised and disorientated, they were all alive. Only John Woravka was missing.

Lady Be Good continued to fly on

alone over the desert long after her men had hit the ground. Her automatic pilot kept her course almost straight and true. With only her right outboard engine running, and despite being on automatic pilot, the plane's nose could be expected to pull to the left and take the aircraft into an ever-decreasing downward circle ending in a messy head-first crash. But *Lady Be Good*'s nose moved only slightly left in a graceful drift for a number of miles before she skidded to rest on the desert floor as if landed by human hands. There she would wait patiently for 15 years for Ronald MacLean to spot her from the air.

15

Day One

MONDAY 5 *April, 1943*
The Liberator finally skidded to a halt some 16 miles south-west of where her crew were gathered in the darkness. They were traumatized and close to exhaustion from their ordeal, but happy and thankful to be alive after leaping from the relative safety of their ship into the terrifying darkness below. Although bruised and battered in body and spirit, they did not at this point believe their lives were threatened. Their attention, such as it was, was focused northwards — they felt they were undoubtedly near Soluch. But the first priority was to locate their missing colleague. They let off a few flares, but Woravka did not appear.

With the benefit of hindsight it has been suggested that the crew should have searched the terrain to the south to find their Liberator rather than heading north. *Lady Be Good* had to be south of them, and carried enough provisions and water on board to sustain her crew for a considerable period. The aircraft also contained an emergency radio with a box-kite to hoist its antenna, which might have helped summon assistance while the men waited in the shelter of the bomber. But this suggestion does not take into account the fact that Hatton and his men were in a state of shock during their first disorienting hours in the desert. They had survived a harrowing ordeal and were not thinking clearly; nor did they enjoy the benefit of hindsight. What is more, the flyers had not heard their bomber crash, nor heard an explosion or seen a fire. They probably believed the aircraft had flown further than it was possible for them to reach. But in all probability, in their confused state of mind the Lady's Men simply didn't think that deeply about the Liberator.

The hour was perhaps 5 a.m., and they had been in the desert for about three hours. It was cold, but the sun was about to rise and it would soon get hot. For the remainder of the day the sun-baked desert would be very hard to take. Hatton and his troops lay on the ground wrapped in their parachutes, awake but motionless. Their bodies ached from stress, and from thumping on to the desert floor when they had jumped. No one had slept: the men were all trying to come to terms with their predicament. Each man was imagining being out there alone in the dark, and wondering what had happened to Woravka. The thought that Woravka's parachute might not have opened was one the men had pushed out of their minds; it was too unpleasant to contemplate. They were also wondering where exactly they were.

Hatton was planning to start the search for John Woravka as soon as the sun rose. His left ear hurt, and he found it difficult to think too far beyond Woravka. He wondered if his ear was infected. His hopes were pinned on a rescue plane appearing with the daylight. Then he wouldn't have to worry or plan any more.

The practical Toner, meanwhile, was thinking that everyone must take an inventory of his gear and determine which items would be useful for desert survival. He also thought about the missing bombardier, and said a silent prayer for him. He was relieved in a way that their mission had been unsuccessful, because his Liberator's bombs had dropped into the ocean and not on people. During the mission briefing the reality that he was about to unload bombs on people had hit him between the eyes. It was almost as if he had never before considered or fully understood the consequences of his position and role in the war. In a matter of hours his point of view had changed. No longer was he taken by the glamour of being a pilot; seen from this new perspective, the business of war now seemed distasteful to him.

Dp Hays castigated himself yet again for landing his friends in such a mess. He had a fair idea of where they were, southeast of Soluch, but he wanted to consult his escape map carefully when the sun came up. Next to him, LaMotte lay speculating on why no one had responded to his radio signals after midnight. He suspected they were a long way from any coastline: at 9.00 p.m. they had been over Naples heading south towards Libya; they jumped six hours later at 2.00 a.m. How could they be near the Libyan coast? He was keeping an abbreviated diary, and considered the possibility of noting his suspicions about their location when the sun came up.

The sun rose over the eastern horizon, and as the air lost its chill the men began to stir. Their stomachs were empty and their mouths tasted rancid with bile. Over the past 15 hours they had eaten very little, having existed mainly on water, coffee, chewing gum and sweets. Hatton and Toner struggled to their feet, followed by the rest of the crew, and tried to focus tired eyes on their surroundings. Slowly they began to comprehend the scope of the wilderness in which they found themselves: a flat, seemingly endless plateau of stones, pebbles and hard sand. In the east the sun was huge, threatening and aggressive in appearance, a big red ball in the sky.

Toner rolled up his parachute, placed it on the ground and lay on top of it. He stretched his aching body, then settled down to write his first diary entry, recalling the events of the previous day:

Sunday 4 April
Naples, 28 planes. Things pretty well mixed up. Got lost returning, out of gas, jumped, landed in desert at 2 a.m. in morning, no one badly hurt, can't find John, all others present.

The reference to 28 planes was incorrect, as only 25 ships from Soluch flew on Mission 109. Perhaps Toner misunderstood his mission briefing, during which everyone was informed that a total of 28 B-17s from the 99th Bomb Group in Algeria would also attack Naples. 'Things pretty well mixed up' obviously suggests a state of confusion throughout Mission 109.

Harold Ripslinger saw Toner recording his entry and proceeded to do the same:

Sunday 4 April
Mission to Naples, Italy. Took off 3.10 and dropped bombs at 10.00. Lost

coming back. Bailed out 2.10 a.m. on desert.

The men cut their parachute harnesses from their shroud lines and threw them in a pile. They had to decide what to keep and what to leave behind. A few threw away their flight boots; some also threw away their Mae West life-jackets. Each man kept his first aid and survival kits, the latter of which contained escape maps, compasses, matches, currency, high-energy concentrated sweets and other provisions. They also retained their parachutes, shroud lines, pistol flares, several flashlights, a few canteens and their meagre personal belongings. Ripslinger and Toner both kept regular diaries, so they hung on to those. Hays and Shelley were lucky enough to have sun-glasses.

Apart from their survival kits, all the men had in the way of sustenance was half a sandwich and half a canteen of water between them. With water so limited each man would be allowed only one capful per day, which should make their supply last four days. By then they would either have been found or made their own way back to civilization, or so they hoped. They immediately drank their first capful of water and began sucking energy sweets. No one gave *Lady Be Good* much thought: the whereabouts of John Woravka was their first concern.

Even in their confused state it did not take the flyers long to appreciate where they had gone wrong. They knew they had crossed the Libyan coast and overflown Soluch while travelling in a south-easterly direction, so the coast must lie to the northwest. Hays was glad that everyone agreed. They were also certain that John Woravka was somewhere to the north, since he had bailed out first, so they had to walk in a north-westerly direction. They had been flying on a heading of 150° before they jumped, and had flown on that heading from the time they contacted Benina — just after midnight — up to the point of the jump, so they decided to begin their march on the reciprocal bearing of 330°. What they didn't know was how far they were from the coast.

Their escape maps showed three trails heading north-northwest from the desert: two starting about 175 miles south-east of Benghazi, and one starting further to the east. But where were they in relation to any of the three trails — east, west, north or south of them?

The men spread out, several hundred feet between each, and started walking north looking for Woravka. From time to time one would call out, 'John, John, John!' Hays was on the western flank, Shelley on the east, and the others in between. Although the sun had only been up for a short time it was already getting hot, so the flyers began shedding but not discarding their leather high-altitude gear. Although encumbered by the things they carried, most of the men had been given a boost by the energy sweets and felt relatively strong.

Hatton was in trouble, however. A sensitive man, the entire ordeal had been too much for him and he was almost spent. The others seemed confident that the situation was under control and covered the ground smartly; Hatton had to struggle to keep up on unsteady legs.

With only the occasional rest stop, by early afternoon the flyers had walked the surprising distance of 19 miles in around seven hours. They had been keeping a look-out for John and listening for the sound of a rescue plane; but John was nowhere to be seen, nor was the sound of an aircraft's engines to be heard. It had become very hot, with heat shimmers in the air, and they could feel the scorching desert floor through their footwear. Unlike most of the crew, who had thrown their flight boots away after landing in the desert, Hays had been wearing both GI shoes and flight boots. Now his feet could no longer take the heat, so he took off his flight boots and placed them on the ground with their toes together pointing north-west. He weighted the boots down with stones to keep the wind from blowing them over.

While discarding his boots, Hays thought he noticed something to his left through the heat shimmer, and went to have a look. He consulted his compass, then shouted to the others through cupped hands: 'Tyre tracks! Tyre tracks over here!' The word passed from man to man, and they quickly closed in on the western flank of the line. Hatton and Toner motioned them to slow down to conserve their strength. In the beating sun almost everyone was beginning to experience trouble with their eyes and lids were starting to close.

The tyre marks were etched along the hard desert sand — a trail of tracks many yards wide running in a north-westerly/south-easterly direction. Their width, depth and location clearly suggested that they had been made recently by either Italian, German or British military vehicles — perhaps five in all. The discovery gave everyone a badly-needed lift, making the men feel that they must be near human habitation. The tracks ran on a bearing of 340°, close to the 330° course the flyers believed they were following. 'What do you think, Bill?' asked Hays of Hatton. 'Shall we follow them?' Hatton consulted Toner, who advised following the tracks, and the rest of the crew agreed. The discovery excited and animated the men, although Vernon Moore was quite matter of fact about the whole thing. He viewed the choice between 340° and 330° as six of one and half a dozen of the other: north-west was north-west as far as he was concerned. He also felt it was too damned hot to follow anything right then.

The temperature was close to 100°F. A terrible heat shimmer rose from the ground around them; they felt their energy starting to sap, and they were dehydrating quickly. For the next few hours they had to shelter. As they had been taught in desert survival training, each man scraped a shallow depression in the sand in which to sit (sand is a poor heat conductor and removing the surface reduced its sting), weighed down one end of his parachute with stones, and held the other end over his head as he sat, making certain that the parachute was always between the sun and his body.

Huddled beneath their silk shelters, their feet baking, their faces blistering, dreading each breath that drew the hot desert air into their lungs, the flyers passed several miserable hours lost in private contemplation. LaMotte remembered the snowy day the year before when his father accompanied him to the air force induction centre in Lake Linden, Michigan, and he swore his allegiance to the United States of America. He remembered how he and his crew proudly boarded their bomber in Topeka, Kansas, and headed off for distant Africa. Things were different then. He returned to the present with a jolt, and his continual nagging suspicion that the others were mistaken to be so confident that civilization was near and help was on its way.

Sam Adams felt his tongue dry and heavy in his mouth and longed for a drink of water. He thought of the town in which he was born, Speedwell in Kentucky: what they needed now was to find a well which would speed water up to them. But of course, there were no wells in the desert, only oases ... He wasn't sure, his mind felt muddled and confused. He pushed the silly thought away and tried to concentrate on his present home, Eureka in Illinois, where since he left the States his wife Dorothy had given birth to their first child. Michael, his son.

In the late afternoon, with no more chance of a rescue plane finding them that day, the men began coming out from under their shelters. The sun was setting, and there was still no sign of John Woravka. Hays thought Woravka had probably found the tyre tracks and followed them north. This made sense to Toner and Hatton, who were certain that if Woravka had been hurt they would have found him by then. Everyone was ready to resume walking, so they gathered their belongings and struggled to their feet. Following the tracks would lead them to safety, but why hadn't a rescue plane found them already? 'It will come,' Toner said. 'Don't worry, it will come. They probably searched the coastal area around Benghazi today.'

Hatton had difficulty standing up, but his mind was clearer than before. He decided to start leaving parachute markers along the tyre trail for the rescue plane to see, putting the first marker a few hundred yards off the trail pointing towards 330°, the group's original route. Hays and Toner laid the arrowhead marker 200 yards east of the trail, weighting it down with stones. It pointed not to 330° but to 325°, the course the flyers were actually following before finding the tyre tracks.

The weary men resumed their north-west trek, walking in single file up the trail. After the sun went down the air quickly started to cool, and with a good breeze blowing from the north-east walking was easier. After a while Moore, who was bringing up the rear, could no longer be bothered carrying his flight boots and shroud lines, so he tossed them on the trail along with a small piece of parachute apparatus. His casual approach to life was never more apparent than here: the equipment was cumbersome so he threw it away, even though the gear might be vital to his survival.

A few miles further up the trail Guy Shelley discarded his leather flying suit, and Hatton put down a second parachute marker not far away. This one pointed straight up the trail on a heading of 340°. Moore, still feeling sick and tired of carrying things, tossed his rolled-up parachute and a section of parachute harness bearing his name at the base of the second marker. Some miles further on Toner put down a third marker, again pointing to 340°, and along this same stretch a few of the men threw away their life-jackets. Everyone was thirsty and filthy; their feet were swollen and throbbing, and they felt on the verge of exhaustion.

It was getting colder, and in the blowing wind Guy Shelley regretted throwing away his flying suit. The men crunched their way up the trail, looking at clusters of stars appearing above them and scanning the desert for signs of Woravka. Every so often someone called out his name. Since dropping into the desert they had seen nothing but a featureless plain: no vegetation, no animals, no birds, not even a cloud in the sky. No Woravka, and no rescue plane.

As the night wore on the group walked and rested, walked and rested. About 15 miles up the tyre trail they put down their fourth parachute marker, having by then walked over 30 miles in 18 hours since bailing out. A few more stumbling miles along the trail several men discarded their shroud lines, and they stopped to rest. Although shivering in the cold night, they could walk no further. They huddled down again, hiding their heads as much as possible from the steadily blowing sand. The dramatic temperature change, the lack of food and water, the stress, the dirt and the uncertainty had all taken their toll. From then on the crew of *Lady Be Good* would need to draw heavily on their courage and faith if they were to survive.

16

Day Two

TUESDAY 6 April, 1943
By the end of the first day the desert had inflicted great damage on the Lady's Men, but it had not broken them; although the crew's strength was draining, their determination was not wanting.

The wind, sand and cold made it impossible to sleep on the night of 5 – 6 April, and by the morning they had neither slept nor eaten much in more than two days. Their eyes were all bad: Robert LaMotte's were almost closed. Ripslinger helped him to his feet while Shelley helped Hatton. In painful stages the remainder of the crew pulled themselves together. The flyers had lost considerable body weight: the normally slight Moore, Hays and LaMotte were shockingly thinner, and the others were not far behind them in weight loss.

Rations for the day were distributed: Ripslinger and Adams shared half a sandwich, the others sucked energy sweets.

Toner sat down again to record his diary entry for the previous day:

Monday 5 April
Start walking north-west, still no John, a few rations, half a canteen of water, one capful per day. Sun fairly warm, good breeze from north-west. Nite very cold, no sleep. Rested and walked.

Ripslinger wrote:

Monday 5 April
All but Woravka met this am. Waited a while and started walking. Had half sandwich and piece of candy and cap of water in last 36 hours.

Still hopeful that the trail they were following would soon lead them to water and safety, they studied their maps. About 200 miles south of Soluch, along what they hoped was the same trail, lay Jalo Oasis. It might be a possible haven, although most continued to think they were near the coast, well north of Jalo. They also clung to the belief that a rescue plane would arrive at any time.

Once again they gathered their gear and prepared to walk. Before starting off Hatton told them that an effort must be made to walk further during the afternoon: their water was quickly declining, and they must wait until the afternoon for their next sip. As they made their way up the trail another man threw away his Mae West. They had been planning to use the life-jackets to store water if any was found. Ripslinger and Shelley still had the presence of mind to keep a look-out for John Woravka, but there was no sign of him.

Hatton was deteriorating badly, although the remainder of the group were holding their own in the tough going. Their pace was slower than the previous day, however, and they were taking more frequent breaks. At 11.30 a.m., having reached the point of diminishing returns, they stopped for a longer rest. Their plans to walk for longer periods during the afternoon were frustrated by the sun, which seemed much hotter than the day before: in the early afternoon they were forced to take cover under their parachutes. The sun was literally cooking them alive; their bodies ached all over, their legs and feet were swollen, and everyone had ugly, bursting blisters on faces and lips.

Guy Shelley is hunched under his parachute, thinking back to Christmas Day, 1932. He was 15 years old and snow was falling. He was sitting cross-legged on the living-room floor in the family home in Bellaire, Ohio, wearing a railroad engineer's cap. Near him was a modestly-decorated Christmas tree; in the background the rich voice of Kate Smith came from a radio, singing that God should bless America. His father sat opposite him in an armchair; his mother was in the kitchen. It was the height of the Depression, and his father was telling Guy how badly he and his mother feel about not being able to buy him the train set he wanted. Young Guy said he understood, he knew times were hard. His father sighed. Only six more days of 1932 were left — it was the end of another bad year in America, and he wondered aloud how many more bad days and years there would be. Guy told his father not to worry. 'You wait and see. Franklin Roosevelt will be President next month, and things will get better.' Then he asked, 'Say, dad, do you think that lost airplane will ever be found, the one called *American Nurse* that flew from America heading for Rome?' Guy's father shrugged. 'I doubt it, son, I doubt it. It was lost ages ago in September.'

Sitting under his parachute Dp Hays was remembering a sunny morning at home in Lee's Summitt, Missouri. His bedroom was small and neat, with everything tidily in its place. A triangular red pennant draped along the wall bore the name of Lee's Summitt High School; a small satchel rested on his bed. Hays stood in front of his mirror putting on his shirt, dressing casually as befitted the summer months of 1941. He talked quietly to his reflection in the mirror as he combed his hair. 'Look at me. I'm 22 years old and I'm going bald. It would be OK if I were tall, but I'm only five foot six. No wonder I can't get a date. And my feet are so small. Hell, there were girls in high school with bigger feet than mine. I weigh 125 pounds: what kind of weight is that for a grown man? And who would name a kid Dp? Just two damned initials for a first name, and even one of them a small letter, small, just like me.' But Dp was happy: he'd got a few days off from the bank where he worked, and was going to St Louis. He wanted to see the St Louis Browns beat the powerful New York Yankees, to see them stop Joe DiMaggio's hitting streak dead in its tracks . . .

The sun sank lower in the sky and the flyers crawled out from under their parachutes, gathering in a circle. LaMotte, Adams and Hatton lay stretched out on their backs, arms folded across their eyes; the rest of the men sat around them. They were exhausted. They were losing weight, every inch of them hurt, and more and more blisters were evident. With the exception of Toner and Hays, who had sun-glasses, everyone had very bad eyes. LaMotte and Moore's eyelids were all but shut tight. Toner heaved himself to his feet and moved around the circle, carefully pouring out one capful of water for each man. Having served the fading Hatton, Toner drank his own capful of water then carefully replaced the cap on the canteen. They didn't have much water left.

In the last 24 hours the men had lost enormous amounts of weight and were having to tighten their belts onto new notches. The two heaviest, Ripslinger and Shelley, were considerably down in size; despite this, Ripslinger still felt surprisingly strong. A few had foolishly stripped to their shorts when the heat was at its worst, which had only hastened the process of burning, blistering and losing body fluids.

By 5.00 p.m. the sun was sufficiently low for the men to resume walking. Ripslinger was helping Hatton, who was in by far the worst condition. LaMotte's eyes were shut tight; Moore, too, had eye problems and Toner was giving him a hand, though he himself needed help. No rescue plane had come and hope for John Woravka had almost disappeared. The men crept their way up the trail. Those able to see with any degree of clarity noticed nothing new; no sign of anything except the same monotonous terrain of hard sand, rocks and pebbles. During a rest stop Ripslinger recorded his diary entry for that day:

Tuesday 6 April
Started out early walking and resting. It's not sundown yet and still going. One teaspoon of water today. The rest of boys doing fine.

After eight more painful miles the flyers put down their fifth parachute marker, and dropped a portion of a sixth parachute next to it. They were by then more staggering than walking, and had only two parachutes left to use as shelters and markers, but they still clung to the hope that help would come or the trail they were following would lead them out of the desert. They pushed on. In two and a half days they had walked 40 miles.

That night the men found they could no longer walk for prolonged periods of time, so they established a pattern of walking for 15 minutes and resting for five. They were growing concerned about following the tyre trail, however, so several miles after putting down their sixth marker Hatton and Toner decided to alter course. They put down a seventh marker in a different place to sound the alarm to the rescue plane that the group intended to abandon the tyre trail: Shelley placed it some 60 feet east of the trail pointing to a heading of 335°. He weighed the marker down with a pair of boots, a small cutting from a shroud line and a portion of a parachute frame, adding a strap from a Mae West by the marker's side.

On leaving the tyre tracks they started walking north-northwest on a heading of 335°, to the west of the trail they had just left. With no tracks to follow they relied solely on a compass heading, but well into the night they were startled to come upon another trail composed of many vehicle tracks — so numerous, in fact, that it was impossible to tell how many vehicles had passed that way. A few gasoline drums were strewn about the tracks, which ran north-east/south-west; the northeast direction pointed towards the coast on a heading of 20°. The flyers felt sure the tracks would eventually intersect with the trail they left some hours earlier, so after careful thought they decided to keep to their north-west course, but on a bearing of 325° rather than 335°. They indicated this change with three markers, using oddments of equipment since their parachutes were nearly gone. The first marker was a section of parachute harness placed on the vehicle trail on a 325°/145° axis; the second was a helmet laid 425 yards northwards on the same heading as the harness. The third, a mound of shroud lines, was put down some 175 yards further on. The ragged group moved on.

By 2.00 a.m., 48 hours after bailing out of *Lady Be Good*, the men felt they could walk no further that night. They needed to rest, and hoped they might be able to sleep a little. Toner, a devout Catholic, led the crew in prayers before they settled down. Until then each man had been saying prayers privately, but the practice of group prayers would continue in the days ahead.

17

Day Three

WEDNESDAY 7 April, 1943 Early morning, and all the men were on their feet ready to walk. They had to cover as much distance as possible before the sun rose and the heat became unbearable. They were little more than walking zombies, and had reached that dangerous point of dehydration where the mind begins to wander and the body slides into shock. Much of their survival gear had been used or lost; there was little left to use as markers beyond shreds of parachute and scraps of equipment.

They had their rations for the day. Little water remained, and, a mere handful of energy sweets. Their clothing was little more than rags hanging from shrinking bodies. The men were unaware of the distance they had travelled; they knew only that they were back following their original course of 325°, and that the first trail was a number of miles behind them. They could no longer walk; instead they stumbled, tripped, and frequently fell. With limp arms and lifeless legs they swayed as if drunk. But on and on they went, step after agonizing step, still believing that the coast was near, that help and water would arrive.

They fed on hope, courage and prayer. The stronger helped the weaker to find the words to pray and the strength to keep going. Toner assisted the almost helpless Hatton; Shelley guided the sightless LaMotte; Ripslinger helped the sinking and blistered Moore. Adams and Hays, limping and bloody-kneed, clung to each other. 'We must keep going, we must keep going,' urged Toner. 'The rescue plane will come, you'll see, it will come.' Hatton went down on one knee, his weight pulling Toner down. Hatton could no longer speak, but Toner managed a croak. 'With me, with me,' he encouraged. With blistered lips Hatton tried to form the words of a prayer, but the sound would not come.

Forward again, on feet like bloody

sponges, licking dry tongues across cracked lips surrounded by pulsating blisters. Hays found a piece of parachute wire in his pocket and dropped it as a marker; Adams weighted down a strip of undershirt with stones; Shelley laid a two-foot section of oxygen tubing on the ground. The sun's glowing face appeared over the horizon, and with this the men collapsed.

Hatton was in a much worse condition than anyone else, and lay sprawled on the ground with his head cradled in Toner's lap. The demands on him had been too much. He was delirious and near death, his eyes mere slits. It was early August, 1942, and he was at Hendrick's airfield in Florida. He was happy: he was learning to fly B-17s, and life was exciting and challenging, so different from sober Whitestone in New York. His sister Elizabeth surprised him with a visit, and they had a lovely day together driving around and seeing the sights. They drove south for about 50 miles to have a look at Lake Okeechobee, where they stopped to drink in the view. He told Elizabeth that he never wanted to be assigned to a B-24 because they were hard for a pilot to jump from — too much distance between the cockpit and the bomb bay.

Hatton's mind wandered again: to Arizona later in 1942, at another airbase. A desert survival course. Sharp male voices shouting 'Yes sir!' in response to an instructor's question. 'Remember, these six rules might save your life if ever you're forced down in the desert. Seek shelter. Find a spot three feet above the ground — it's always cooler there. Never undress. Keep motionless. Collect your urine — one cup will give you three hours' life. Move only when the sun is down. Remember, at 15 per cent body dehydration your mind will start to go. At 18 per cent you won't be able to speak or swallow. At 25 per cent you're damned near dead. So obey these rules and avoid dehydration. Remember, you dehydrate faster with your clothes off. Do not take off your clothes during the day in the desert. I say again, taking off your clothes in the desert during the day is off limits!'

Something was troubling Hatton, fretting

at the edge of his mind. Yes, that was it: his mother Rose. His adviser, his friend, the one he always turned to when he had problems. The one he would worry about most. The one he would share most news with in his many letters. The one he wrote to first when he flew solo:

Well, Mom, today is a memorable day in my life. After 14 minutes in the air Larry Silkey got out of the front cockpit, after we had made our landing, and said, 'Well, Hatton, she's yours for the next 20 minutes.' Mom, it is customary to take off, fly around the field and land three times on a solo flight. I had a few minutes left over so I did it four times. When I taxied over to where Silkey was standing, he grinned, reached over the edge of the cockpit with his extended hand and said: 'That was good, Hatton.' It was the first time he's complimented me on anything. Hope everything is going well at home, Mom, and I wish all of you could be half as happy as I am right now.

After helping Hatton through this difficult period Toner somehow found the strength and clarity of mind to record his diary entry for the previous day:

Tuesday 6 April
Rested at 11.30, sun very warm, no breeze, spent p.m. in hell, no planes, rested until 5 p.m. Walked and rested all night, 15 minutes on, five off.

For the rest of the morning the crew inched their way north-northwest, stopping frequently to rest. In the early afternoon the sun became too intense for them to go on, and they sheltered again under what little remained of their parachutes. The difficult hours passed slowly. All hope of finding John Woravka had disappeared, but hope of a rescue plane finding them still persisted, at least in the mind of Robert Toner. He continued to listen for the sound of engines.

When the sun went down the men once again got to their feet, which in itself was a miracle. They had already dehydrated more than 25 per cent, and according to scientific theory should be turning on each other like wolves by now. But far from attacking each other, they managed to keep going throughout the evening and most of the night. By the time they collapsed again they had walked 20 miles since leaving the first trail, an astonishing distance given their physical condition, and a total of 65 miles from their bail-out point.

18

Day Four

THURSDAY 8 April, 1943
Another day was beginning. Once again the sun was on the brink of rising and more searing heat was on the way — not the answer to the crew's prayers. The men were up again on their wobbly legs and moving. They looked indescribable, more dead than alive, and it was incredible that they kept going. They were driven on by the belief that they must be near the coast: they weren't sure, but at one point during the night they thought they heard birds overhead. It might have been their imagination, but if they were right the coast could be near.

Before setting off Toner and Ripslinger faithfully recorded their diary entries for the previous day. Toner's diary set the standard: his handwriting and clarity of thought had hardly varied since his first diary entry, and would continue to remain consistently lucid. His example and thinking greatly influenced the crew's movements and behaviour in the desert, though each man in his own way displayed inspiring courage. Toner wrote:

Wednesday 7 April
Same routine, everyone getting weak, can't get very far, prayers all the time, again pm very warm, hell. Can't sleep. Everyone sore from ground.

Ripslinger had his own version, complete with several revealing details:

Wednesday 7 April
Started early am and walked 'til about spent. Terrible hot afternoon. Started again 6 p.m. and walked all night. One spoonful of water is all.

That day the flyers had to contend with an old adversary: another sandstorm, a small sister of the sandstorm which had plagued Mission 109 and helped to get them in their present predicament. The storm lashed into their backs, blowing northwest in the same direction in which they were walking. Swept and buffeted by wind and sand, Shelley noticed through nearly closed eyes a deviation in the terrain — a fairly high knoll. He thought it might also attract the attention of a low-flying rescue ship, and those who were still coherent agreed it would be a good spot on which to place their eighth and last parachute marker. Shelley, one of the few men with enough strength left, climbed the knoll and put down the marker pointing towards 325°, weighing it down with a few stones. While he was thus engaged, one of the others mistakenly dropped a face-mask made from parachute silk in which two holes for the eyes had been cut out.

The crew hobbled along again, trying to protect their gaunt faces from the wind as best they could while continuing to cling to one another. Everyone was tripping and falling, but after every fall they would struggle up once more. Those still upright helped the fallen back onto bloodied, swollen feet so painful that their ankles would hardly support them.

Few of the men could speak any longer, and those who could found the task made more difficult by blowing sand intruding into their throats and lungs. Hatton, LaMotte and Adams passed out more than once, but were brought around by their comrades. The Lady's Men were in agony and their bodies ached from pain and fever.

Even under these brutal conditions the men made good progress during the early morning hours, but the intense afternoon heat again forced them to stop. Virtually all their equipment had been thrown away or used, and their last small portion of parachute was barely enough to provide shelter for one man. The flyers sprawled out on the ground at the mercy of sun, sand and wind.

The honourable Bill Hatton was in a shocking state, as near death as it was possible to be. Blowing sand had penetrated his lungs, just as it had done in Virginia Beach two years earlier. Toner wondered if his friend would survive the day, and also if a rescue plane would ever come. He and the others were painfully aware that the rescuers had had more than ample time to find them.

Sam Adams, too, was near death: he was badly dehydrated and his mind was wandering. He remembered how he came to be part of Hatton's crew just five months previously; had it not been for that odd twist of fate, he would never have been in this situation. All of a sudden, in January, 1943, he was elevated to the rank of staff sergeant and assigned to Hatton's crew as tail gunner after the original gunner disappeared during Christmas, 1942, and couldn't be found; and that was why he was in this fix today. It was all that tail gunner's fault.

LaMotte's mind was somewhere else, too, wandering and fading in and out of reality and consciousness. He was back in March, 1942, again, on that cold, snowy day in Lake Linden, Michigan. He was going to join the air corps, and his whole family were there to bid him farewell and good luck, to hug him and kiss him and cry their Italian tears. His mother, his father, his sister, his five brothers: they all wanted to be there on the day Robert joined Uncle

Sam. His father told him the whole family was proud of him, and that soon most of his brothers would follow him into the service. He hoped the training would not be too tough for his son, and that God would look over him and protect him wherever he was sent. But his father had mixed feelings about America having to fight Italy, saying Mussolini would never be forgiven by Italians for getting Italy into the war. The Italian people never wanted war with anyone, much less war with America. LaMotte assured his father that he would be OK, that everything would turn out well for the Italian people, and that the family should not worry about him.

The situation for the lost flyers was becoming desperate. All but Toner had lost faith that a rescue plane would ever come, and only Ripslinger and Shelley had any degree of life still left in them. Given what they had been through, the two men's stamina remained amazingly high and they could still see reasonably well. Toner was almost physically spent, but with great difficulty he could manage to speak. He gathered the crew around him in a rough circle and tried to boost morale. They had their water for the day, just a few drops, and listened to Toner croaking. The situation was critical. Their water would soon be gone. John Woravka was lost. Probably only God could help them now. But he still had hope that a rescue plane would find them.

Toner asked everyone to join him in a prayer: 'Oh God above, watch over us. Grant us the courage and strength to go on. Light the way for John Woravka. Send help if that be your will.' He then asked the crew to say, or think if they could not manage to speak, the words of 'Our Father', and the men complied within their failing capabilities. Finally, Toner recited a 'Hail Mary'.

For the rest of the afternoon the men lay still, pounded by the wind, sand and sun. Somehow, as the sun went down, they once again got to their feet and continued north-west, walking and resting, walking and resting. By nightfall the ground underfoot was changing: it was no longer hard with stones and pebbles, but soft, loose sand which made the going even more difficult than before. During one of their rest stops Toner wrote his diary entry:

Thursday 8 April
Hit sand dunes, very miserable, good wind, but continuous blowing sand. Everybody weak, thought Sam and Moore were all gone, everybody else's eyes are bad. Still going north-west.

The lost flyers did not know it, but they had already walked some 70 miles. Toner's comment, 'Hit sand dunes', was probably one of hopeful anticipation rather than fact. At this point in their struggles the flyers were about 18 miles from the northern perimeter of the plain which marks the beginning of the Calanscio Sand Sea, labouring through a constantly shifting carpet of wind-blown sand. The ground underfoot had altered so sharply from gravel to sand that Toner probably believed they had reached the dunes at last. It is noticeable that Ripslinger makes no mention of sand dunes in his diary entry for that day:

Thursday 8 April
Tired all out. We can hardly walk our fourth day out. A few drops of water each. Can't hold out much longer without aid. Pray.

19

Day Five

*F*RIDAY *9 April, 1943*
The sun had yet to rise, but the moribund crew had been creeping onwards throughout the night. They had stumbled, tripped, fainted, collapsed, recuperated and rested, with the wind knifing into their backs the whole time. They should have died long ago, but this gritty bunch of ordinary men had pushed on, armed only with their stubborn courage. Physically the Lady's Men were down to little more than bones covered with blistered, leathery skin; their faces were tight masks out of which wolf-like teeth protruded. They had reached a point of depletion where they were fainting as a prelude to death. It was no longer a case of the strong helping the weak, more a matter of the near-lifeless helping the zombies. The line between the two was thin.

They were all blind except for Ripslinger, Toner, Moore and Shelley. They had survived for four days, in temperatures which at times had reached over 100F, on just a few capfuls of water each. Almost everyone had given up hope that a rescue plane would find them, and each man must have realized long since that they were nowhere near the coast. What these extraordinary ordinary men didn't know was how to give up. They could so easily have stretched out and died, but still they kept on going.

With the desert bathed in early morning light the Calanscio Sand Sea lay in the distance for those with eyes fit enough to see. The crew trudged towards it through soft, windblown sand. By late morning they had walked about 78 miles from the bailout point. The sun's heat was unbearable. Hatton, Toner, Hays, LaMotte and Adams were so beaten that they could no longer continue. They tried their best, but even with help their rubbery legs and balloon-like ankles succumbed and they fell face first into the sand. Only

Ripslinger, Shelley and Moore still had any strength at all. Moore had proved to be amazing: the previous day he had apparently been blind and near death, but by the morning he was at least as vital as the exhausted Ripslinger and Shelley. The three tried to assist their fallen friends, contriving a modest shelter for them with what little parachute silk remained. Each man was given a few drops of water, although they had so little left that no one could do much more than wet his lips.

Moore, Ripslinger and Shelley were left unprotected, taking the full impact of the sun's rays. Ripslinger prayed silently for mercy, and the word made him think of his sister, who was a nun with the Sisters of Mercy congregation. When he last saw her, she and her congregation said they would always pray for him and his crew. He remembered embracing her on the day he left home to join the air corps in 1942.

Ripslinger's thoughts travelled further back in time, to a warm, sunny, autumnal day in 1938. He was playing in a football game at high school in Saginaw, Michigan, racing down the field carrying the ball, weaving in and out, shedding tackler after tackler. He scored a touch-down, and the spectators cheered. Then there was a day in America shortly before they left for North Africa. He was at Topeka Army Air Base in Kansas, and the crew were having a group photograph taken by the tail of a Liberator. LaMotte, Ripslinger, Moore, Shelley and Adams knelt in front; Toner, Woravka, Hays and Hatton were standing. The photographer said, 'Everybody smile,' and the camera clicked.

More recently, there was the night he sat drinking coffee with the other sergeants in the NCO club at Soluch, the night before Mission 109. All the other men in the club were drinking beer or wine. Ripslinger was talking to a sergeant at the next table who had the peak of his cap turned up, asking him questions because the sergeant, Byers, had already been on two missions. He wanted to know how to avoid enemy flak, and Byers just said that you couldn't, but that if you could hear the flak then it was too damned close. Then Byers said that what was killing everyone wasn't so much the flak as the haemorrhoids. Everyone who'd been on missions had them, and Ripslinger's crew would get them too. The field hospital was full of guys having haemorrhoids cut out. Everyone got them from the constipation caused by stress and punishment to the body on long missions in temperatures of 20°F and 30°F below zero. Then Byers added that if you urinated in the fuselage tube the damned stuff froze in your hand the moment it left your body. And Ripslinger remembered Byers saying that he was writing his experiences in a diary: he was going to immortalize the 376th Bomb Group after the war if he survived.

His thoughts returned unwillingly to the present as he sizzled in the sun and wondered if he and his friends would survive. And with this, being a devout Catholic, Ripslinger decided to lead Shelley and Moore in a prayer to the Mother of Mercy. The rest of the crew were almost incoherent, but perhaps they could hear and take comfort from the words.

The walking was over for five of the crew, and for the rest of the day they all waited; waited for a rescue plane that would never come.

20

Last Days

*S*ATURDAY 10 April, 1943
At some point during the night of 9 April or the morning of 10 April, Ripslinger, Shelley and Moore left the rest of the crew and began stumbling towards the Calanscio Sand Sea in search of help. The trio were driven by the belief that Soluch lay on the other side of the Sand Sea. They had flown over a chain of such dunes south of Soluch airfield during their familiarization flights when they first arrived there, and prayed that the hills of sand within their sights were the same ones.

The Toner and Ripslinger diaries fail to agree as to when the three men left, but it was probably on 9 April. For this date Toner wrote:

Friday 9 April
Shelley, Rip and Moore separate and try to go for help, rest of us all very

weak, eyes bad, not any travel, all want to die. Still very little water. Nites are about 35°, good north wind, no shelter, one parachute left.

Ripslinger's diary implied that the men were still together:

Friday 9 April
Fifth day out and we all thought we're gone. All wanted to die during noon it was so hot. Morn and nite OK. Two drops of water!

At this stage in his ordeal it is likely that Ripslinger's mind was crumbling, with Catholicism acting as his only remaining safety net. He probably believed that the Lord had led the crew to the dunes, beyond which lay salvation. In their prayer meetings Ripslinger and the rest of the crew, especially the Catholics, must have been highly conscious that they were in the Lenten period leading to Holy Week — spoken of by ancient writers as the Week of the Holy Passion, the Penal Week, and the Week of Forgiveness. As a devout Catholic, Ripslinger must have been struck by the similarity of their predicament with that of Christ in the period leading up to the crucifixion, including fasting and suffering in the wilderness.

In his confused state, however, Ripslinger believed that Saturday 10 April was the end of the fifth week of Lent, so Sunday 11 April would be Palm Sunday. Palm Sunday was very much on his mind: it marked the beginning of Holy Week, and was thus important to him. But in fact Easter Sunday fell on 25 April, 1943, so Saturday 10 April was the end of the fourth week in Lent and Palm Sunday would be on 18 April.

When Ripslinger and his companions separated from their friends they went empty-handed. Any remaining dribbles of water were left with the dying men. Half mad from thirst and hardly able to stand the three set off towards the dunes, which they could only just see but which they believed to be near. Little did they realize that the dunes, which looked huge, were all of ten miles away. But crossing them was their only hope; their only remaining chance to save themselves and their friends. They stumbled on through the night and when the sun came up they were still going. A light wind was blowing, and the men were more than half dead. During a rest stop Ripslinger still had the presence of mind to write up his diary:

Saturday 10 April
Walked all day and night. Suggested Guy, Moore and I make out alone.

The three airmen travelled on for ten miles across a terrain of soft sand, each painful step like wading through glue. On finally reaching the dunes they breached them through a valley and somehow managed to go on, finding strength and determination from some unimaginable source. By the end of the day Ripslinger, Shelley and Moore had travelled an incredible distance with no food or water. Twenty miles to the south Toner wrote:

Saturday 10 April
Still having prayer meetings for help. No sign of *anything*, a couple of birds;

good wind from north. Really weak now, pain all over, still all want to die. Nites very cold, no sleep.

After recording this entry Toner fell on his back. He and the others were little more than skeletons. Toner reflected on the irony of his situation, remembering how badly he wanted to become a pilot. It was early 1940, and he was on a rocky beach in New England. Low-flying seagulls were swooping over the choppy waters diving for fish. It was a windy day, and Toner was sitting on a rock with his older sister Gertrude watching the seagulls and talking. Toner told his sister that they just didn't want him. 'I want to get into the war but my own country won't have me. So I've joined the Canadian air force — they need all the help they can get.' Gertrude said she understood, that she knew how disappointed he must be, but that he must remember America was not at war. 'It's only a matter of time,' he replied.

Now it was 1942, and he was in a US Army Air Corps recruitment office in New England. An officer was seated at a desk behind which stood a limp American flag; on the wall was a photograph of President Roosevelt and a poster of Uncle Sam. Uncle Sam's right arm pointed straight forward, his forefinger extended from his fist below the words 'I Want You'. Toner sat opposite the recruitment officer, neatly dressed in winter clothes. The officer studied Toner's application papers and said, 'We turned you down before because your school grades were only average. Since then I see you've been busy: you qualified with the RCAF, you have more than 200 flying hours, you're highly motivated. That's good, we like that. Uncle Sam can use you now America is at war. There is just one thing, though — you will have to learn to fly all over again. The Canadians teach you their way, we teach you ours.'

Bill Hatton had been pleased when he learned he was getting the experienced Toner as co-pilot. Toner remembered the day several weeks earlier when the crew first arrived at Soluch. Toner, Woravka and Shelley were in their tent; the others had gone out. Toner and Woravka were sitting on the same bunk, with Shelley on another bunk opposite them. They were writing messages for cables to send home, but their messages must be brief. Toner had already written his, and Shelley was suggesting a sentence to Woravka. 'You say it your way, I'll say it my way,' replied Woravka. 'I'm going to put, "Please don't worry." It's going to my brother Alex.' Shelley's cable was for his parents. It said, "All well and safe."

Another 24 hours passed, but by 11 April Toner, Hatton, LaMotte, Adams and Hays were only barely alive. They were still frying in the merciless sun. Toner wrote:

Sunday 11 April
Still waiting for help, still praying, eyes bad, lost all our weight. Aching all over, could make it if we had water; just enough left to put our tongues to, have hope for help very soon, no rest, still same place.

The hopes that help would arrive in the near future illustrate the men's belief that Soluch was just beyond the sand dunes. Toner expressed no concern for the well-being of Ripslinger, Shelley and Moore, so he presumably thought they had already reached safety, or would do so very soon. After everything he had endured, Robert Toner's clarity of thought and penmanship is truly astounding. He was still totally in control mentally, and clearly had not given up hope.

More than 20 miles to the north, Ripslinger, Shelley and Moore trudged on through the dunes. Ripslinger made another entry in his diary:

Sunday 11 April
Palm Sunday. Still struggling to get out of dunes and find water.

Ripslinger would write nothing more. He and his two friends reached the crest of a dune and disappeared behind it. When they appeared again only two were left. Little by little and one by one the sun was finishing the three men off. Some miles further on and deeper into the dunes only one man remained: probably either Shelley or Moore. Some

Robert F. Toner's diary entries for Sunday, April 4, through Monday, April 12, 1943.

SUNDAY, APR. 4, 1943

Naples — 28 planes — things pretty well mixed up — got lost returning, out of gas, jumped, landed in desert at 2:00 in morning, no one badly hurt, can't find John, all others present.

MONDAY 5

Start walking N.W., still no John, a few rations, ½ canteen of water: 1 cup full per day. Sun fairly warm. Good breeze from N.W., nite very cold, no sleep. Rested & walked.

TUESDAY 6

Rested at 11:30, sun very warm, no breeze, agent P.M. in hell, no planes, etc. rested until 5:00 p.m. walked & rested all nite. 15 min. on, 5 off.

WEDNESDAY, APR. 7, 1943

Same routine, every one getting weak, can't get very far, prayers all the time; again P.M. very warm, hell. Can't sleep. every one sore from ground.

THURSDAY 8

Hit Sand Dunes, very miserable, good wind but continues blowing of sand, every man very weak, thought Sam & Moore were all done. La Motte & squad gone, every one else's eyes are bad. Still going N.W.

FRIDAY 9

Shelly, Rip, Moore, desperate & try to go for help, rest of us all very weak, eyes bad, not any travel, all want to die. still very little water. Nites are about 35°, good N. wind, no stars, & parachute left.

SATURDAY, APR. 10, 1943

Still having prayer meetings for help. No signs of anything, a couple of birds; good wind from N. — Really weak now, can't walk, pains all over, still all want to die. Nite very cold. no sleep.

SUNDAY 11

Still waiting for help, still praying, eyes bad, lost all our wgt, aching all over, could make it if we had water; just enough left to put our tongue to, have hope for help very soon, no rest, still same place.

MONDAY 12

No help yet, very cold nite.

TUESDAY, APR. 13, 1943

WEDNESDAY 14

THURSDAY 15

Harold S. Ripslinger's diary entries for Monday, March 29th, through Sunday, April 11, 1943.

WEEK BEGINNING

MONDAY Still No plane And Still in Town. Sleeping Late in Morning, Having Nice Showers And Eating Nice Meals With lots of Fruit

TUESDAY Boy o'boy! What A Vacation. I Bit The Boys At Camp Are Really Envious We Cracked Cyl. on Eng Saw A Movie Tonight Swell!!!

WEDNESDAY PLANE Still Not Ready But CAME Back in Another B-24 The Boys Were Glad To See Us & Visa Vera. Nice Trip

MARCH 29th. 1943

APRIL 1ST

THURSDAY Nice Sleep last Nite Got Up To late for Breakfast. Went To Confession And Communion!!! Nice Going Rip!! We're Going To Have Mass Everything

FRIDAY Nothing Much Doing To day. Shelley & Sam Got Their First letter, oh Boy!!! Some Got paid Too. Mine Was Wrong Won 45.00 in CARDS.

SATURDAY Nothing Exciting Today. Sam Got 5 letters. I'm Waiting My 1st from Gert Saw Show Candy Tonite

SUNDAY Mission To Naples Italy To. 3:40 And Dropped Bombs at 10:00 Lost Coming Back. Bailed Out At 2:10 A.M. on Dessert

WEEK BEGINNING

MONDAY All But Wojravka Met This A.M. Waited Awhile & Started Walking Had 1/2 sand which piece of candy & cup of Water in East 36 hr. !!!

TUESDAY Started out Early. Walking & Resting It's Now Sundown & Still Going. One Tea Spoon of Water Today. The Rest of The Boys Are Doing Fine.

WEDNESDAY Started Early Again. & Walked Til About Noon Spent Terrible Hot Afternoon Started Again at 6 P.M. & Walked All Night. One spoon Full of Water is All

APRIL 5th. 1943

THURSDAY Tired all out. We can Hardly Walk our 4th Day out. A Few Drops of Water Each. Can't hold out much Longer Without Aid. Pray!

FRIDAY 5th Day out & We All Thought We're Gone. All Wanted To Die During Noon It Was So Hot Make it nite o'kay. 2 Drops of Water!

SATURDAY Walked All Day & Night. Suggested 'Guy' Moore & I make out Alone

SUNDAY Palm Sun. Still Struggling To Get out of Dunes & Find Water

267

miles after that no one was left. All three were dead.

On Monday 12 April Robert Toner recorded his last diary entry. It is highly likely that everyone with him was still living at the time, although all their water had gone. Toner wrote:

Monday 12 April
No help yet, very cold nite.

By Tuesday 13 April all the Lady's Men were dead. The first to die was probably William Hatton, who on 20 October, 1942, while with the Second Air Force in Salt Lake City, Utah, awaiting a posting had written to his mother:

There are about four places they can send me. Arizona, Idaho, and Spokane or Tacoma, Washington. I am sitting here waiting to see which one it is. I hope it isn't Arizona because I am tired of sand.

21

Oilmen Again

LIKE CBS's Armstrong Circle Theatre story on 2 February, 1960, the Fuller/Neep report of 17 November, 1959, concluded with the opinion that *Lady Be Good*'s crew had perished in the Calanscio Sand Sea, and their remains had probably been covered by sand. The investigators from the US Army Mortuary System had done everything humanly possible to recover the bodies of William Hatton's crew: no amount of time, effort or expense had been spared in the four-month search which concluded early in September, 1959. As far as the American news media, the military authorities, the public and the relatives of the bomber's crew were concerned, that was the end of the sad story of the Liberator with the stylish name.

Then, on 11 February, 1960, only nine

days after the CBS show, a discovery was made some 78 miles north-west of where Hatton and his men had bailed out. A water-well drilling team owned by the Canadian company Geoprosco, a D'Arcy Exploration subcontractor, was working in a desert area near the southern boundary of the Calanscio Sand Sea; an area which was once part of Application 121, later known as Concession 81. The Canadians stumbled upon the remains of what they felt certain were the bodies of five of *Lady Be Good*'s missing crew.

By then most oilmen working in Libya were well acquainted with the aircraft's story and the huge American attempts made the previous year to recover her crew's remains. Almost every D'Arcy man whose work had taken him near the bomber's crash site had visited the Liberator in search of souvenirs, and the plane's body was rapidly being stripped. The general view among the oilmen was that the American investigations had been exaggerated, wasteful and highly public relations oriented.

The finding of the five dead crewmen

was an unhappy occasion for Jim Backhaus, the Canadian team manager. He and his men were saddened at the sight of the pathetic skeletal remains, closely grouped in an area littered with canteens, flashlights, pieces of parachute fabric, flight jackets, shoes and other bits of equipment and personal belongings. Hatton's effects consisted of a gold wedding band inscribed 'Love to W.J.H. from A.J. 9-3-42', two religious medals, one comb in a leather case, and a three-bladed pocket-knife. There was a case for sun-glasses, inscribed inside with the name Dp Hays. And, of course, there was the poignant diary of Robert Toner, describing what had happened to the crew and how three men had left the others and gone in search of help.

The remains at the site were eventually positively identified as being those of Lieutenant William J. Hatton, Lieutenant Robert F. Toner, Lieutenant Dp Hays, Sergeant Robert E. LaMotte and Sergeant Samuel R. Adams.

On the same day as the Canadian discovery, Captain Richard Dolezal piloted his Silver City Airways Dakota into

Concession 81 with water and other supplies for the Canadians and a nearby D'Arcy seismic crew. Jim Backhaus took Dolezal to the site of the remains. On flying away from Concession 81 later that day, Dolezal sent a radio message to Silver City's Tripoli office reporting the discovery, and Silver City relayed the news to Wheelus Air Base.

The next day, 12 February, Silver City's Captain Charles Hellewell, who had piloted Ronald MacLean when *Lady Be Good* was first spotted from the air 20 months earlier, flew a Bristol freighter aircraft into Concession 81 with more supplies for the D'Arcy oilmen. On landing he was met at the strip by Backhaus, who asked if Hellewell had heard about the discovery and would like to help with a superficial identification of the remains. Backhaus had ensured that nothing at the site had been disturbed and that the area was being treated with respect. The two men drove the short distance to the site in a Land Rover, and Hellewell vividly recalls what they found:

I can still remember the shiver that went down my back looking at the scene. For some reason it looked so peaceful, and I remember thinking surely some of the answers lie here. Most of the remains were eroded by sand and wind but the first object I saw was a USAF-type empty sunglasses' case partly eroded. The name Lieutenant Hays was written inside. We had decided not to touch anything but in looking for ID tags I gently with a finger scooped sand from around the neck of one body and found just below the surface hair and skin still intact. I stood up and quietly walked away, thinking 'There but for the grace of God go I'. It was an emotional moment for me: these were fellow airmen 17 years ago and the conclusion for me of a mystery brought about by a chance flight almost two years earlier.

The body from around whose neck Hellewell scooped sand was that of William Hatton. By coincidence, as a 19-year-old RAF cadet Hellewell had arrived for training in Clewiston, Florida, on 8 August, 1942. Hatton had arrived at Hendrick's Air Base, Florida, on either 7 August or 8 August, 1942, also for training. Hatton and the pilot who eventually helped spot his crashed bomber had trained a mere 60 miles apart.

The finding of the five bodies and the Toner diary, with its indication that three of the crew had separated from the group and continued toward the dunes, triggered the US Army Mortuary System's second major search for the remainder of the crew. Operation Climax would be concentrated north of where the remains had been found and, as before, large amounts of equipment and manpower were employed.

From experience gained during the 1959 operations it was known that a combined air-ground search using helicopters guided by vehicles would be the only practical method. The degree of American military commitment to Operation Climax was astounding. Enormous volumes of equipment were airlifted from Frankfurt in Germany to Wheelus Air Base, and from there airlifted again into the desert about 80 miles north-west of *Lady Be Good*, where it would be convenient for the various phases of the search operation and close to a suitable water supply. Investigators Fuller and Neep recorded details of the equipment:

Two K-13 helicopters with spare parts and tools

One ¼-ton truck with an aircraft homing device and sand plates

Two ¼-ton trucks with AN-GRC-9 radio, compass and sand plates

Two ¾-ton trucks with AN-GRC-19 radio and dual rear wheels and sand plates

One ¾-ton truck with AN-GRC-19 radio, dual rear wheels and sand plates [sic]

One small field kitchen with messing facilities for 23 people.

Tentage, tent flies, tables, chairs, lister bags [purpose unknown], field cots, air mattresses, sleeping bags, tools and lumber, an initial supply of water and motor fuel in 55-gallon drums.

The search party itself was equally impressive:

One search commander/navigator
One assistant commander/navigator/
   identification specialist
Three grave registration specialists
Four helicopter pilots
Two helicopter maintenance specialists
One topographical specialist
One radio operator/repairman
Two drivers/motor mechanics
Three drivers
One mess sergeant/first sergeant.

They were accompanied by an army public information group including one photographic control officer, one motion picture service operator, one stills photographer, and one public information writer.

The planning and execution of Operation Climax lasted from February until the end of May, 1960, but as late as 14 May, despite all their efforts and much to their embarrassment, the American investigators had still not found any more of the crew's remains.

The wording of Toner's diary was perceived as a source of problems by the leaders of the investigation team. At first Captain Myron Fuller refused to release the diary's contents to the public: such personal effects are normally considered to be the inviolable property of the next of kin. Instead of the exact wording, Fuller permitted a paraphrased statement to be issued to the press from the Wheelus Air Base information office on 18 February, 1960:

Entries in the diary indicate that only five of the nine members of the crew died at this location. One failed to join the party after bail-out from the bomber, and three later left the group to continue on ahead for help. No positive personal identification has been made, but experts of the US Army Mortuary System were said to indicate the members of the group being recovered were First Lieutenant William J. Hatton, pilot; Second Lieutenant Robert F. Toner, co-pilot; Second Lieutenant Dp Hays, navigator; Technical Sergeant Robert

E. LaMotte, crew member; and Staff Sergeant Samuel R. Adams, crew member. The tentative identifications are indicated from diary entries, and from such physical evidence on the spot as dog tags, an identity book, an Air Corps ring and other personal effects.

Captain Myron C. Fuller, of Placerville, California, head of the mortuary team, said that the personal account found indicated that the man who failed to join the party after bail out was Second Lieutenant John S. Woravka, bombardier, and that the three who left the main group were Technical Sergeant Harold S. Ripslinger, Staff Sergeant Guy E. Shelley, and Staff Sergeant Vernon L. Moore. These diary indications eliminated the possibility that other bodies would be found in this immediate location. It had been previously thought the remains of other members of the crew might be buried in the sand nearby. Bail-out time was established by the diary, which indicated that the five men in the group being recovered reached this location on 9 April, five days after bail-out. The last entry in the book was 12 April, but the exact date of death is unknown.

For millions of American citizens who had followed the wrenching story of *Lady Be Good*, it simply was not good enough for someone thousands of miles away to tell them what Toner's diary 'indicated' to him. They wanted to read the words themselves and come to their own conclusions. It seemed to many an intolerable case of the military withholding information for no good reason.

The Pentagon was set upon by the news-wire services, *Life* magazine, several national news services, and the producer of the Armstrong Circle Theatre, who had travelled from New York to Libya in order to present the story accurately on television. Quick to react to public sentiment, on 20 February, 1960, the Pentagon ordered that the wording of the diary be released by Wheelus Air Base. In a last effort the army censored two small phrases: 'all want to die' and 'still all want to die'. This may have been to spare the feelings of the crew's relatives, or perhaps because the army thought that American soldiers should display an invulnerable and immortal attitude even when on their last legs, at least as far as the public were concerned. But the news media were so outraged by this censorship that the Pentagon was forced to send out further orders, directing that the diary's precise contents be released immediately. *Life* magazine was able to print the full wording of Toner's diary in its issue of 7 March, 1960.

At that time a handful of oilmen, most of them British and all in the employ of BP's subsidiary D'Arcy Exploration, had played an important role in helping to bring the story of *Lady Be Good* to light. With the exception of the search for the plane made by Don Sheridan, John Martin and Gordon Bowerman, most of the discoveries had been accidental. In May, 1960, two more D'Arcy oilmen were to join the exclusive group of 'finders': Don G. Livingstone and David W. Glover. Both had heard all about the discovery of the aircraft from Bowerman and Martin directly. They knew about the first abortive attempt by US investigators to find the crew's remains, and were also aware that a second attempt was currently in progress after the Canadian discovery of five of the crew.

Born in Cambridge in England and educated at Cambridge University, Don Livingstone had taken up a land surveying career with a firm of civil engineers and had worked for two years on the Volta River hydro-electric project in Ghana. He joined BP in 1956 to work on seismic oil exploration parties in Kuwait, and after two years there moved to Libya and BP's D'Arcy Exploration. In 1960 he was 30 years old. David Glover was born in 1926 in Great Missenden, England, and sprang from a family of flyers: his father had flown with the Royal Flying Corps during the First World War, and his two older brothers with the RAF in the Second World War. A transport engineer by profession, as a teenager David Glover had served in the British army during the later years of the war. He joined BP in Tanganyika in 1956 and was posted to D'Arcy in Libya in 1958.

The 1959 ground survey conducted throughout Application 121 by Sheridan, Martin and Bowerman resulted in the belief that oil reserves might lie hidden beneath the flat northern plain of the application. By early 1960 Application 121's southern Kufra area had been returned to the Libyan Petroleum Commission and its northern stretch registered as D'Arcy Exploration's Concession 81. There was a great deal of D'Arcy activity there at the time, as the company had plans to drill an exploration well in the general vicinity of the *Lady Be Good* crash site.

Meanwhile, to the north-west of Concession 81 and on the western side of the Calanscio Sand Sea, about 150 miles from the crash site, D'Arcy had set up a materials and transport camp called Lulu Field in a stretch of desert known as Concession 80. To make significant improvements to the logistics of moving large drilling equipment round and south of the Sand Sea from Concession 80 to 81, it was proposed that a route threading through the Sand Sea directly from one concession to the other be reconnoitred. Dave Glover, D'Arcy's transport engineer, and Don Livingstone, in his role as a surveyor, were appointed to find such a route.

The Calanscio Sand Sea consists generally of roughly parallel lines of dunes oriented in north-northeast/south-southwest directions. The dunes usually slope gently on their western flanks but have steep slip faces on the eastern sides, making approach by vehicle or foot from the west generally easy but approach from the east very difficult. An individual dune line will vary in height along its length, with the occasional lower saddle where it is sometimes possible to drive through and then return.

Glover and Livingstone were travelling from west to east in their attempt to plot a route through the dunes. Their procedure was to drive up the west flank of a high dune and search north and south with binoculars for a possible break in the dune-line, to which they would then drive and hopefully get through. They were plotting their whereabouts on aerial photos of the area. Proceeding in this zig-zag manner Livingstone and

Glover had taken a few days to get from Concession 80 to the more open area of Concession 81. They were aiming for the vicinity of the Geoprosco water-well site, whence it was easy driving into the main body of Concession 81.

During the late afternoon of 11 May they came up against another long line of dunes, and Livingstone climbed to its summit to search for a suitable way through into the next valley. Just before leaving the summit Livingstone noticed a small white sphere at the base of the dune's steep east face. His first impression was that he had at last found a whole ostrich egg; many oilmen had found pieces of ancient ostrich eggs in the area but never a whole one. In the neolithic era the whole region had been savannah grasslands, and flint arrowheads and other artefacts had been found in addition to egg fragments.

Livingstone called down to Glover saying he thought he had spotted a virtually complete ostrich egg. Glover wasted no time in scampering up the western face of the dune to join his partner, and both then slithered down the east face of the dune. Their ostrich egg was a skull. They would later learn that it was the skull of Guy Shelley. Together with the skull were most of the rest of Shelley's skeletal remains, shreds of uniform, and the unmistakable shoulder badge of a Second World War US airman. For the two oilmen the unhappiest part of their discovery was a pair of boots, from which the remnants of feet and leg bones protruded. Alongside the remains were a lighter and wallet, which the oilmen later handed in to the US search team. The wallet contained local currency which crumbled to dust when taken out, a laundry list belonging to Ripslinger, and a photograph of a man in the uniform of an American airman.

Standing over Shelley's remains, Livingstone and Glover had deep feelings of sadness that someone so determined should have suffered such a cruel fate all alone so many miles from anywhere. They thought perhaps it was better that the ship's crew did not know they had virtually no chance of walking to safety from their bail-out starting point. In describing the site where

Shelley's remains were found, David Glover said:

From the top of the dune where we found him, and looking north in the direction in which Shelley was going, all he would have seen to the very horizon would be lines and lines of dunes. It is possible, I think, that having struggled up to the top of the dune, and having seen what was ahead of him, Shelley was probably overcome with the impossibility of walking much further. Sergeant Shelley must have been very weak at this time.

The next day Glover and Livingstone reached the water-well site on Concession 81 and contacted the American investigation team searching nearby. The two oilmen then accompanied the investigators back to Shelley's remains. According to the second Fuller/Neep report the map co-ordinates of the site were 28° 10′ N, 23° 05′ E, placing Shelley's remains 37.5 miles on a bearing of 305° from where the other five bodies had been discovered. The amazing Guy Shelley had walked at least 115.5 miles from the bail-out point on perhaps six capfuls of water and virtually no food beyond a few energy sweets.

The finding of Sergeant Shelley prompted the American investigators to carry out an air search for the remains of Moore and Ripslinger along a line bearing 305 from the site where the five remains were found to the Shelley remains 37.5 miles to the north-west. Nothing more was sighted during this search.

On 17 May, 1960, two years to the day after *Lady Be Good* had first been spotted from the air, the remains of Sergeant Ripslinger were found on the eastern slope of a high dune at map co-ordinates 28° 05′ N, 23° 13′ E. Although the second Fuller/Neep report is a little unclear as to exactly who found him, the person (referred to in the report as the 'observer') was almost certainly part of the US search team.

Ripslinger was 26 miles from the five-man site, also on a bearing of 305°. His remains were almost completely buried in soft sand with only a small area of the skull, right shoulder, a few ribs and the right hip exposed. Unlike Shelley, Ripslinger's remains were intact, lying on the left side with legs drawn up slightly and both arms positioned with the hands near the face. Mummification had taken place except where the body was exposed. Technical sergeant chevrons on the sleeves of the wool olive-drab shirt and a diary found in the pocket clearly suggested that the remains were those of Harold Ripslinger. He had walked at least 104 miles from the bail-out point. After Ripslinger's death Shelley had walked an additional 11.5 miles.

The final American search operation to recover the remains of Sergeant Moore was conducted over the same area as that searched on 17 May when Ripslinger was found. Having discovered the remains of Shelley and Ripslinger on the eastern slopes of high dunes, the investigators felt it likely that the remains of Moore and even perhaps Woravka were to be found in similar circumstances. Although the investigators had now completely covered the area it was decided to make one final attempt with special attention being given to the eastern slopes of the dunes. The 26-mile stretch to where Ripslinger was found was again searched with high hopes of finding Moore, who, according to Toner's diary, was apparently in a weaker condition than either Shelley or Ripslinger and would probably have fallen along this stretch. The dunes were carefully scanned, but without success. By the end of May the search was brought to a close and the investigators left Libya, never to return.

The Fuller/Neep report of 20 June, 1960, to the commanding general in Washington concludes:

Remains number 6 and number 7 were designated SR5053 and SR5054 and taken to the identification laboratory of the CM Mortuary System, Europe, for final processing and identification. All the area surrounding the courses followed by still missing Second Lieutenant John S. Woravka and Staff Sergeant Vernon L. Moore have been thoroughly searched. From evidence found at the sites of the two recovered remains it is evident they were alternately covered and exposed on numerous occasions by the windblown sand. The still missing remains are apparently sufficiently covered by sand at this time so as to escape detection.

Still the story of *Lady Be Good* would not rest: on 11 August, 1960, Wheelus Air Base received yet another message from D'Arcy Exploration. A seismic party working close to the plane's crash site had discovered the remains of another American airman at co-ordinates 26° 54′ N, 24° 08′ E; probably those of Lieutenant John Woravka. It was indeed the bombardier. The discovery was made because there were so many tyre-tracks up and down in the areas where work was in progress that the oilmen kept driving more and more to the east of the trail to avoid driving over old tracks and sinking into soft powdery under-sand. In the process they drove right past Woravka's remains. He was lying face up with his parachute piled on top of him, clothed in his flying suit and Mae West. It was obvious from the tangled shroud lines around him that his parachute had failed to open. His death on impact finally explained why Woravka had not joined up with the rest of his crew.

The Mortuary System personnel from Frankfurt had by then long since returned to Germany, but on receiving news of Woravka's discovery they wired Wheelus with instructions that the base flight surgeon should recover Woravka's remains from the desert. Pilots Rubertus and Pinkston therefore flew Flight Surgeon Cada to the Woravka site and the grim business of recovering his body began.

John Woravka's body was lying some 16 miles north-east of *Lady Be Good*. The unexposed portions of his remains contained flesh; parts of his body had yet to dry out and the ground under him was damp from body fluids. Attached to Woravka's clothing was a canteen still three-quarters full of water despite lying exposed to the sun for 17 years. To remove Woravka's remains from the desert, pilot Bill Robertus gently took him by the feet while Flight Surgeon Cada tended to the shoulders. In lifting him, Woravka came apart at the knees — every bone was broken. Without clothing the bombardier weighed 72 lbs.

In one of Woravka's shirt pockets was a blank notepad, which passed through many hands after the remains were discovered. It was not until a very long time after he was found, perhaps years later, that someone noticed the pad was not completely blank: on one page three questions had been written (see chapter 8). It is the only known record of anything written during *Lady Be Good*'s flight. The three brief sentences were probably Woravka's way of communicating with Dp Hays while the men were on oxygen without using the intercom, and confirm the view expressed in Toner's diary record of Mission 109 that the whole flight was confused and things were 'pretty well mixed up'.

Since the recovery team was to be near the Liberator's crash site, it was decided before leaving Wheelus that they would also recover the ship's propellers. The team included a mechanic to help with this task. While being driven from the Woravka site to that of *Lady Be Good*, the Wheelus men came upon a pile of parachute harnesses, discarded flight boots and expended signal flare cartridges. These marked the spot where the crew of *Lady Be Good* had assembled after bailing out: prior to this discovery no one really knew where the crew had actually rallied after hitting the desert floor. The distance between this point and the Woravka site was around four-tenths of a mile.

Vernon Moore's remains have never been found, and with the finding of John Woravka the mystery of *Lady Be Good* and her crew was thought to be closed. But eight years on a new and totally unexpected twist would be added to the tale, joining all the other little unresolved questions connected with the bomber's saga.

22

Mystery Projectile

THE twist in *Lady Be Good*'s tale was a half-inch fragment of a two-inch long 20 mm projectile discovered in the port inner engine. Was this proof that the Liberator had been attacked by an enemy fighter during Mission 109? No serious account of the aircraft's story would be complete without examining in detail the steps leading to the discovery of this mystery projectile.

In 1968 the British still operated an RAF base at El Adem, near Tobruk on the Libyan coast. In that year the American McDonnell-Douglas Corporation of St Louis, Missouri, was eager to obtain parts of *Lady Be Good*'s engines and other samples from the aircraft for analysis. They wanted to study the engine for signs of sand and climate damage, especially the cylinder heads. But the prominent aerospace firm was unable to persuade the Americans at Wheelus Air Base to make yet another trip to the wreckage of *Lady Be Good*, so they approached the RAF in El Adem.

In January, 1968, the commanding officer of the base received a letter from James W. Walker of McDonnell-Douglas. Walker, a sales engineer, requested that if the RAF ever conducted a desert rescue exercise in the general vicinity of *Lady Be Good* they would consider recovering and bringing back to El Adem specific samples for environmental tests by McDonnell-Douglas. In March the RAF acceded to this request and, after gaining diplomatic clearance from the Libyan government, a nine-man desert rescue team set off towards the crash site to collect the samples in between navigation exercises in the near-trackless wastelands of central Cyrenaica.

The expedition began on 12 April, 1968, and concluded on 22 April — and none too soon at that, because in September, 1969, Colonel Muammar al-Qaddafi overthrew Libya's aged King Muhammad Idris al-Mahdi al-Senussi and, prompted by Libya's close relationship with the Soviet Union, proceeded to kick both the British and American military out of his country. Since then Libya has been a no-go area for most British and American people other than media representatives and, not surprisingly, oilmen and their families: some 10,000 expatriates in one way or other connected with the oil business reside in Libya today.

On 24 May, 1968, Flight Lieutenant Adolph P. 'Zeke' Zeleny, navigator and officer in charge of the desert rescue team, submitted his portion of the lengthy report dealing with the visit to the *Lady Be Good* crash site. The aims of the exercise had been to train the team in desert driving, Sand Sea crossing, navigation and locating a target without aircraft cooperation; to prepare and mark a landing strip; and to collect parts of the B-24 aircraft for McDonnell-Douglas. Their brief did not include recovering an entire Liberator engine weighing thousands of pounds — that would have been too much for McDonnell-Douglas to ask for or expect.

This extract from Zeleny's report deals with the general desert terrain in which *Lady Be Good* lay:

The *Lady Be Good* Basin (for want of a name). This is a roughly circular area of 100 miles in diameter, bounded by the Libyan Sand Sea (or Calanscio Sand Sea) as named on some maps, on the east, north and west. In the south the basin is bounded by a nameless group of mountains, which isolate it from the Kufra plain. [The basin is] like an enormous airfield covered with brown gravel and firm, coarse sand of whitish colour. The whole plain is criss-crossed with many tracks in every direction and different markers abound. The regular pattern of seismic explosions is found frequently, usually marked by posts. The basin seems to be devoid of any growth, though an odd solitary dried bush was occasionally seen. On the western side of the basin is a solitary chalk rock aptly named Blockhouse Rock (27° 02′ N, 23° 31′ E) which serves as a good fixing point. The rock itself is a haven for migrating birds, and both exhausted and living and dead specimens were found at the rock. There must be a considerable number of snakes around, judging from the amount of discarded skins, and the resident hawk flew lazily away upon the approach of humans.

At the wreck of *Lady Be Good*, though no vegetation was found for miles around, there is a quite large animal colony. The wreck and its surroundings are infested with mice, which obviously feed on the remnants of the food left behind by the various visiting expeditions. The mice were quite tame and a nuisance during the night, running across one's face or forever rummaging in one's belongings. There were two spotted lizards living in the broken-off engine. A large animal, probably a stoat, was observed in the fuselage during the night, and its paw marks ranged all over the camp. There were pellets left probably by an owl, which was not seen. There were three swallows playing around, and a very shy wheatear, a pretty black and white bird. The king of the roost, a bird of prey, whose perch was a sagging wheel of *Lady Be Good*, cleared off as soon as the team approached.

In another section of the same report, Flight Lieutenant B. Sellers, deputy leader of the desert rescue team, gave a technical assessment of the condition of the aircraft and items removed for dispatch to St Louis:

Position and Environment
Lady Be Good (B-24) lies on a flat sand/gravel plain, co-ordinates 26° 42′ N, 24° 02′ E [slightly wrong]. The plain is terminated to the north (100 miles) and to the east (40 miles) by a sand sea. The surface of the plain consists of small pebbles and gravel. Under this lies both sand and gravel. Typical daytime temperatures on 17 – 19 April were of the order of 20 – 30°C. Accurate observations taken at 1400 hours local on 19 April were: Dry temperature 25.4°C, wet temperature 14.8°C, relative humidity 30 per cent.

Condition

The aircraft has lain in its present position for 25 years. During this time it has been extensively 'plundered', presumably for souvenirs and for items for research. The tail and rear half of the fuselage are separate from the remainder, and lie at a small angle to the fore and aft axis of the remainder. However, it is believed that the tail has been dragged to this position from a more remote one.

The lower part of the front portion, including the bomb bay, is buried in sand. This sand is difficult to dig away due to the congestion and confined working space within the shell.

The four engines were found lying in their correct relative positions, but separated from the wings. Little was left of the starboard inner engine, but the other three were more or less complete.

The remains of the aircraft were in excellent condition considering the environment. Control surfaces such as the port aileron (which was still complete except for the surface skinning) still moved freely.

The port undercarriage is in the fully retracted position within the wing, and the mainwheel cover appears to be in almost mint condition. The starboard undercarriage lies at a shallow angle to the mainplane and again is well preserved.

Removal of Specimens of Material
The major item removed and brought back to El Adem is the port inner engine. This was loaded, without major hitch, in about one hour onto a three-ton lorry, using the windlass of two of the Land Rovers. This was the easiest of the three almost-complete engines to load as it was completely severed from the aircraft. It was not buried in sand, as was the lower portion of the port outer engine.

It was hoped that the port aileron would also be complete, but the inboard hinge defied removal, either by removing the aileron from it, or the hinge from the trailing edge of the wing. After two hinges had been released, therefore, the aileron was cut across about six inches outboard of the inboard hinge.

To provide further samples of skin and paint, the following were also removed:

a. Deflector plate from the starboard side of the fuselage.

b. Inspection panel and portion of surface from the port mainplane.

Rubber samples were obtained from the following positions:

a. De-icing boot from the port mainplane leading edge root.

b. Two oxygen tubes, one of which was lying free from the aircraft in full sun, the other of which was taken from a relatively shaded place inside the cockpit.

c. Rubber floor step covering.

d. Rubber beading from astro-dome.

e. Sample from starboard tyre. It was not possible to remove the complete wheel and cover.

f. Sample from starboard flexible fuel tank.

Two plexiglass panels were removed from the front of the cockpit. One was broken as found, the other complete.

It would be very much appreciated if it were possible for items such as cylinders, pistons and con rods to be returned to El Adem, after the engine has been stripped and research completed.

Lady Be Good's specimens were flown from El Adem to St Louis in a complicated operation co-ordinated from St Louis by James Walker. He contacted the USAF Museum in Dayton, Ohio, who arranged for the US Air Force to provide transportation from El Adem. The engine would become the museum's property, on loan to McDonnell-Douglas until their tests were complete.

On arrival in St Louis the engine and a few of the aircraft's other specimens eventually found their way not into a spacious McDonnell-Douglas hangar or laboratory, but into the small garage at James Walker's home in Florissant, Missouri. There, for a number of years, Walker carried out a series of corrosion tests on the sand-crusted engine. The USAF Museum eventually took possession of the engine during the 1970s after other McDonnell-Douglas tests had been completed.

In the course of these later examinations, on a date unknown to the author, a small half-inch fragment of a 20 mm projectile was found lodged inside the thin metal rocker-box cover on top of the engine's number one cylinder. The discovery of a cannon projectile of that calibre was curious, as the bullet fragment could probably only have found its way into the Liberator's engine as a result of attack by an enemy fighter plane. The projectile must have entered the open cowling on the front of the engine, ricocheted inside and come to rest in the rocker box. To the author's knowledge, no damage of any kind was done to the ship's engine by the projectile fragment other than piercing the thin rocker-box cover.

Of all the little mysteries connected with the *Lady Be Good* story, the appearance of this projectile fragment in the bomber's engine is by far the most puzzling. It is also the least significant, because the projectile appears to have had no effect whatsoever on the engine's performance during Mission 109.

Although many will be more than justified in disagreeing, the author finds it very difficult to accept that *Lady Be Good* was indeed attacked by an enemy aircraft at any time during the mission. The reasons for this belief are so numerous that the question is begged as to whether or not the projectile fragment entered the engine by means other than attack.

Consider these points. Why was only a fragment of the projectile found in the engine, and not either all or other parts of the projectile? What happened to the rest of the projectile? The average 20 mm bullet is about two inches long, and its total mass could not have been reduced to half an inch without a trace of other parts nearby. Why was no collateral damage done to the engine other than the primary piercing of the rocker-box cover? A 20 mm projectile entering an engine must do so with terrific force.

Why is it that no outer or inner part of *Lady Be Good* showed any sign of battle damage when found? There were no rips or bullet-holes in her skin. Why especially was there no battle damage of any kind done to the nose section of the bomber, particularly near the cockpit, port inner wing edges or any surfaces of the aircraft close to the port inner engine? Other than normal propeller buckling on the bomber's numbers one, two and three engines, all of which were feathered when the Liberator hit the ground, there is no evidence that a bullet may have hit or scraped the propeller of the port inner engine or the propellers of any other engines. No mention of this type of damage has ever been made by McDonnell-Douglas to the author's knowledge.

What is more, why is it that neither the diaries of Robert Toner and Harold Ripslinger nor an abbreviated third diary kept by Robert LaMotte make any mention of an attack? Why is it that no log mentions it either? Why, if an enemy fighter attacked *Lady Be Good* once, did it not attack again?

Arguments in favour of the attack theory are no less compelling than those which question if an attack ever actually took place. *Lady Be Good* had never been in combat prior to Mission 109. She only had 148 hours on each engine prior to her first mission, and most of these hours were clocked up in the USA, so the likelihood is that the mystery projectile was acquired on Mission 109. Based on the angle of the entry point, and considering that no mention is made in any diary or log of an attack, if such an attack took place it must have occurred at night, and not much later than around midnight while *Lady Be Good* was near the Libyan coast and all four of her engines were running. Her crew may not have been aware of the attack. The likelihood of a projectile finding its way through a spinning propeller, although remote, is a possibility.

The Junkers 88 which Colonel Compton probably thought was in the Benghazi area around midnight on 4 — 5 April might indeed have been the attacking plane. The problem with this theory is that the engines of only one aircraft were heard after 11.30 p.m. that night — all other Liberators had been accounted for by that hour. If an enemy aircraft did attack at night, it probably did so having stumbled upon the Liberator by airborne radar (carried by Ju-88 night-fighters) and the attacker may have been unable to locate the bomber again for another attack, or the attacking plane may have been low on fuel and had no time for a second attack.

If *Lady Be Good* was not attacked, the question remains as to how the mystery projectile came to be in the bomber's port inner engine. Many remote possibilities come to mind, but nobody can answer this question with any degree of certainty. Nor, probably, will the puzzle of the 20 mm projectile ever be solved.

There are other nagging loose ends in the story of *Lady Be Good*, but unlike the matter of the curious projectile there is a chance that one or two of these may be resolved in the not too distant future. It is still unknown who actually gave the Liberator the name *Lady Be Good* just a few days before Mission 109. Then there is the question of how a letter addressed to a Sergeant Shea came to be in the Liberator. No one by that name appears to have been connected with the 376th Bomb Group during the period concerned.

How is it that the unmanned *Lady Be*

Good, almost without fuel and running only on her right outboard engine at low altitude, managed to fly level for almost 16 further miles after her crew bailed out, veering only slightly east, and perform a text-book belly landing rather than crashing head first into the desert? Why was Robert Toner, a man with some 700 flying hours, not the pilot of his crew rather than William Hatton, who had only about 500 flying hours? How is it that the remains of Vernon Moore were never recovered, when the probable area of his death was repeatedly searched?

Why is it that Dp Hays' navigator's log was not found for, at the very least, 16 months after *Lady Be Good*'s discovery? The oilmen who located her do not recall seeing it when they went through the ship. The first Fuller/Neep report, dated 17 November, 1959, has this to say on the subject:

There was no trace of the Navigator's Log for the flight of 4 April, 1943, but one log sheet fragment was found concerning an earlier training flight.

The final Fuller/Neep report, dated 20 June, 1960, makes no mention of finding a log. The RAF's 'Report on Desert Rescue Exercise', dated 24 May, 1968, nine years after *Lady Be Good* was found, says nothing about finding a log. Yet at some point someone found it.

The author acquired a copy of the log in 1985, having previously been unaware of its existence because, to the best of his knowledge, no mention had been made of it either verbally or in print. The author had not at that time seen the Fuller/Neep report, and was unaware that enlarged copies of the log and *Lady Be Good*'s radio data sheet were mounted on the wall of the US Air Force Museum at Wright-Patterson Air Force Base in Dayton, Ohio. The documents have been specially treated to prevent their deterioration.

When, how and from whom the museum acquired these documents is unknown to the author. But the questions of who exactly found them, and when, pale into insignificance in comparison with other unresolved points. After the navigator's log was found, did the authorities have it analysed? Has this log ever been analysed? And if so, what conclusions were reached? These questions are important because if the log has been analysed the authorities cannot have failed to conclude that on Mission 109 *Lady Be Good* was a long way from Naples at 7.45 p.m. If this conclusion has ever been reached, why has it not been made public? The author is not aware of any announcement along these lines, and to this day supposedly knowledgeable people believe that *Lady Be Good* was in the Naples area at about 7.45 p.m. This was certainly not the case.

Could a few of the entries in Toner's diary have been written by another member of the Hatton crew? In reply to a letter from the late Elizabeth Henry, Hatton's sister, dealing with the matter of Hatton's personal effects, the office of the quartermaster general in Washington, DC wrote on 10 May, 1960:

The diary and an address book which belonged to Lieutenant Robert F. Toner, the co-pilot of the plane

Lady Be Good, were found in the pocket of a shirt near Lieutenant Toner's remains. From the written entries in the diary it appeared certain that it belonged to Lieutenant Toner; however, as an added precaution both items were forwarded to the Federal Bureau of Investigation for a comparison of the handwriting. The Bureau reported that while not all of the handwritten entries were suitable for comparison, the conclusion was reached that the majority of the handwritten entries in the diary and the address book were written by the same person. Accordingly, the diary, along with other personal effects, was forwarded to Lieutenant Toner's next of kin.

The allegation that Hatton made a voice-call at around midnight which was heard in the Benghazi radio tower is something which, to the best of the author's knowledge, has never before appeared in print, although many have been aware of this claim for years. The thrust of Hatton's call, if indeed it did take place, was that he needed a position report because his automatic direction finder (ADF) was not working; in other words his radio was working but his radio compass was not. For years it has been said that when the American investigators first went to the *Lady Be Good* crash site they found that her ADF radio compass worked perfectly. The Fuller/Neep report made two relevant observations:

> The radio set of the B-24 was removed and installed in the SC-47 where it worked perfectly in place of the radio which had failed on the flight from Wheelus Field . . .
> The radio compass was set to 311.0 KC for 'homing'.

It is noteworthy that the report says the radio compass was set for homing, not that it was in working order.

In the interest of accuracy a few words must be said about the matter of distances walked by Hatton's crew, as well as other relevant distances derived from the Fuller/Neep reports. They may not be totally accurate; some distances may be less than thought, others may be more. An example of the latter is the distance between the crew/Woravka bail-out point and *Lady Be Good*. For years this distance has been said to be 12 miles; in fact it is more in the order of 16 miles. This can be confirmed by plotting the two relevant co-ordinates on a good map with precise latitude and longitude lines. The first co-ordinate is 26° 54′ N, 24° 08′ E, the crew/Woravka bail-out point; the second co-ordinate, that of *Lady Be Good*'s position, is 26° 42′ 45.7″ N, 24° 01′ 27″ E as fixed by Gordon Bowerman. If this relatively short distance is incorrect then other greater distances given in the Fuller/Neep report may very well be wrong. But rather than querying exactly how far Hatton's crew walked, suffice it to say that every man covered an enormous number of miles with very little sustenance in appalling circumstances.

There is no question that on landing in the desert most of Hatton's crew felt they were near the coast. The evidence of their north-west walk proves this. Yet at least one crewman guessed that they had landed not near the coast, but in a location about 30 miles from where they actually came down. Whether the guess was made at the beginning, middle or end of the crew's walk will probably never be known. But such a guess was indeed made, because one of the silk escape maps found along with the crew's remains had a pencil hole punched in it some 30 miles from the crew's actual bail-out point.

The hole was spotted by accident many years after the map was found — perhaps 15 or 20 years later — and was detected by James Walker of McDonnell-Douglas when he held the map up to the light for close examination. Until then, although the map had passed through many hands, no one had ever unfolded it, since it was one of many identical maps found in the desert belonging to Hatton's crew. Walker came by the map through a small American military museum and, on contacting those through whose hands the map had passed, he was assured that the map had never been unfolded up to the time he acquired it. The likelihood of such a hole being punched in the map at that particular location by anyone other than a Hatton crewman is highly unlikely.

The saga of *Lady Be Good* and her crew is the tragic account of unfortunate men. No doubt scores of similarly unusual incidents took place in past wars and are unknown. *Lady Be Good*, or at least what remains of her, still lies in the Libyan desert 440 miles south-east of Benghazi where Don Sheridan, John Martin and Gordon Bowerman found her 35 years ago. Various attempts in America to return the aircraft to her rightful place have failed, and the US government officially abandoned the Liberator in 1962. The remains of the ship's crew have been laid to rest in more appropriate places:

William J. Hatton — Long Island, New York

Robert F. Toner — North Attleboro, Massachusetts

Dp Hays — Arlington, Virginia

John S. Woravka — Cleveland, Ohio

Harold S. Ripslinger — Saginaw, Michigan

Guy E. Shelley Jnr. — Harrisburg, Pennsylvania

Robert E. LaMotte — Lake Linden, Michigan

Samuel E. Adams — Eureka, Illinois.

Vernon L. Moore still lies in the Libyan desert.

The crew of *Lady Be Good* died bravely and needlessly no more than six weeks after the photograph on the dust-jacket of this book was taken. One can only hope that these men and the spirit of their stripped aircraft rest in peace.

23

Final Thoughts

IN Chapter 6 the discussion concerning the identity of the mystery lead Liberator which turned away short of Naples concludes that it was probably aircraft number 37, piloted by Lieutenant Brian Flavelle. It was also noted that Second Lieutenant Guy Iovine's ship was flying immediately ahead of Flavelle's bomber. The two pilots, who were close friends, both landed at Malta, but the question is still begged as to why Flavelle turned. In the estimation of the three pilots who were following him towards Naples, Flavelle's Liberator appeared to be operating normally at the time. Two of them also comment in their sortie reports that there was sufficient daylight left to bomb the target. There was nothing to indicate any problem, nor any apparent reason for Flavelle to turn away.

This incident has been commented on

in the past within the context of the belief that the ship which turned away from the target was *Lady Be Good*. However, quite apart from the clear evidence to the contrary found in Hays' navigator's log for Mission 109, other clues as to the lead Liberator's identity and the reason for Flavelle's strange behaviour can be gleaned from the infamous Ploesti bombing mission in which the 376th Bomb Group participated.

In the weeks following the disappearance of *Lady Be Good*, 'attack' was the operative word in and around Benghazi for the 376th and other bomb groups. Something big was brewing: a major low-level attack on an unknown target. The mission's codename was Operation Tidal Wave, and when details were eventually forthcoming it transpired to be an assault on an important source of German petroleum: a tidal wave which would engulf Ploesti in Romania on 1 August, 1943.

A third of the Third Reich's fuel supplies during the Second World War came from the oilfields at Ploesti, but in the early days of the war the region was virtually out of range of Allied bombers. An American air attack launched on the area out of Egypt in June, 1942, had failed; Operation Tidal Wave was intended to succeed, and would become the most famous single Liberator action of the whole war.

The operation was planned on a much larger than normal scale, with 177 bombers and around 1,700 airmen taking part in the attack. They would take off at dawn on a long-distance raid designed to take the enemy by surprise. Had *Lady Be Good* and her crew survived Mission 109 they would undoubtedly have participated in the Ploesti raid, but (with the exception of John Woravka, whose broken body lay nearly 90 miles to the south) they had long been lying lifeless in or near the Calanscio Sand Sea by the time the multitude of airmen assembled in the chill morning to prepare for take-off.

One of these airmen was Dick Byers, flying on board a Liberator named Little Richard in his honour. In his diary Byers recorded the tension of the day preceding the attack, and the unforgettably brutal Ploesti mission itself:

Saturday 31 July, 1943
The ships are being checked again and again. Special delayed-action bombs are being installed in the bomb bays. Some are 500-pounders and a few of the newer ships are carrying 1,000-pounders. Boxes of incendiary sticks are being placed by the waist windows. They weigh about 20 lbs each. Pick them up, the spring snaps to go, and she blows in about 20 seconds. The delayed-action bombs are from one to six hours. The last ships over the target area are dropping bombs to explode on impact. This is cutting it pretty close.

Last-minute briefings have been going on all day. The combat crews are isolated totally from all non-flying personnel. Guards are all over the place. You'd think it was a prisoner of war camp. General Bereaton, commanding the Middle East bomber forces, spoke to us on the importance of the mission and why it must not fail: thousands of lives will be saved and the war could be shortened by six to 12 months. Its effects on the enemy war machine would be felt immediately. General Ent, commanding the Ninth Air Force, also addressed the group. He is flying the mission with us. Colonel Compton, commanding the 376th, also spoke. Later in the day the head of the British air force, Air Marshal Tedder, addressed the group. Eddie Rickenbacker told us of his Pacific experiences and wished us Godspeed. To top it off, General Bereaton closed by saying, 'If not one bomber returns and the target is totally destroyed, it will be worth the sacrifice in men and bombers.' A great morale builder for all the combat crews.

Most of us have already accepted that we'll lose at least 50 per cent of the striking force. The groups coming down from England to assist us no longer refer to this theatre of war as 'bombing milk runs'. After the mission they will be returning to England. The long-range B-24 will make this mission one for the history books, and flyers for years to come will discuss this controversial raid.

In a few hours we'll be on our way.

We'll be flying *Little Richard*, number 2-40660, and Colonel Compton's *Teggy Ann*, carrying General Ent, will be just off our left wing. My squadron, the 513th, is leading the 376th, and the 376th is leading the other four groups involved. The 98th will be directly back of us. Our ship will be number five to take off; there will be only four ships in front of us.

There will be no sleep tonight. The crews participating are gathering the items they want sent home. These are placed at the head of the bed. At the foot of the cot are the items the survivors can take and share amongst themselves. Maybe these items will make their day-to-day existence more bearable. The security officer told us that we could write one letter home, seal it, give it to him, and if we didn't make it back he would mail the letters uncensored. My letter is addressed to my mother and inside is a letter to my wife for my mother to mail.

Tension is at its highest level. The countdown seems to be under way. God willing, I'll be here tomorrow night to record the events of Sunday 1 August, 1943. It's an honour to be a small part of this historic undertaking that could change the course of the war. Our crew, I'm proud to say, all stepped forward to volunteer. There was no question in anyone's mind. If we don't make it back, this diary will be given to Captain Huntley and he has been requested to send it to my wife in Minnesota.

It's 3.00 a.m. on Sunday morning, 1 August. We've stuffed our pockets with candy, gum, cigars, cigarettes. If we're going to crash, we want some of the comforts. Even took a few beers along. They have given us flak protectors made of woven steel, which should stop bullets and flak. They look like a baseball umpire's protective front: very heavy and restricting movement. My guess is we won't wear them and take our chances with bullets and flak. Breakfast is at 3.30 a.m.; something like the condemned man's last meal. Best we've had since February.

Everyone had an opportunity to attend a brief religious service of his choice. Believe me, there are no non-believers going on this mission. We all made our final peace with God. The expressions on the faces of these young men said a great deal. Your life seems to pass by. Thoughts were of home and loved ones, and also of the grim task ahead. No one spoke. Just silent reflection.

The trucks immediately took the crews to the ships. When we arrived the ground crew personnel stood in front of the ship. We passed by, shaking hands. Nobody spoke. They could see the determined looks on our faces. They knew nothing concerning the target to be bombed. They immediately left in the truck. We grimly shook hands with the crews adjacent to our ship. Then we shook hands with each other and boarded *Little Richard*.

In a few minutes we will start engines and taxi out into position. After weeks of training and preparation the moment has arrived. The success of this mission will largely depend on whether or not we can take the enemy by some degree of surprise — get in and out. Hopefully we'll be back to record the events. God willing, we will.

Sunday 1 August, 1943
The target was Ploesti. Five major refineries in and surrounding the Ploesti area. Almost 14 hours in the air. The historic events of the day are almost beyond imagination and belief. If the story was fiction, the reader would say, 'A fantastic imagination in story-telling; beyond belief.' But it's all true. The mission to Ploesti was written in sacrifice, blood and death from the beginning.

As the sun began to rise, 177 planes built to bomb at high altitude started taking off from five airstrips surrounding Benghazi. At Benghazi the 376th and 98th had asphalt runways. The three other airstrips were just bulldozed out of the desert for Liberators from the Eighth Air Force. Blowing dust there from bombers taking off presented serious delays in take-off. *Little Richard* was the number five ship off from Berka 11 strip. Ships immediately flew over the desert and into specific locations as quickly as possible. The ships were overloaded with over 3,200 gallons of high-octane gasoline and at least 4,400 lbs of bombs, plus a huge quantity of 20 lb spring-activated incendiary sticks. All ships were carrying extra belts of 50-caliber bullets, armor-piercing, incendiary and tracer shells.

The Ninth Air Force was well represented. The 376th Bomb Group, headed by Colonel Compton's 'Liberandos', had 28 ships. The 98th, headed by 'Killer' Kane's 'Pyramiders', had 47 ships in formation. Then, especially over from England for Ploesti, the Eighth Air Force had 39 ships from the 'Travelling Circus' group headed by Addison Baker; Leon Johnson's group, the 'Eight Balls', had 37 ships in the air; the 'Sky Scorpions' headed by Jack Wood sent up 26 ships. That made 177 bombers in all.

The target, Ploesti, is about 1,000 miles distance and deep in enemy territory. We're going unescorted, as fighters haven't the gas capacity for such a journey. The Russians could have given us air cover, as Ploesti can't be more than half an hour from Russia. None came, and the high command instructed the crews that we couldn't under any circumstances fly a crippled bomber to Russia. If you are forced to crash-land, do so in enemy territory — not Russia. We could have carried twice the bomb load and half the gas if we could have proceeded to land in Russia after bombing Ploesti. Strange, as Russia is supposedly our ally.

The 98th had an overloaded bomber roar off the end of the runway, overturn and explode. No survivors! A huge column of smoke rose into the sky — a warning of events to come. Time could be running out for over 50 per cent of the striking force. About an hour into the mission the lead ship with the best navigator, flying about ten feet off the Med, crashed, broke into two pieces and sank immediately — no survivors! The group circled, looking for swimmers, but none surfaced. Shortly afterwards we flew directly over a German U-boat charging its batteries. Most of the crew was diving off the sub and swimming. We should have bombed and sunk her as she no doubt sent an urgent radio message: some reference to 'huge bomber formation heading in north-east direction'.

The island of Corfu near Albania, just south of the Straits of Otranto, was our first navigation check-point. The Mediterranean was still, like a huge mirror: no white-caps, and very peaceful. I'm sure most of us wished we could have been elsewhere. As we headed through the mountains of southern Yugoslavia, heavy cloud cover caused the formation to spread out and become separated. The 98th was behind us, the other three groups from the Eighth Air Force were about 45 minutes behind the 98th. They had problems getting off the ground because of blowing sand and dust.

After literally going through the mountains, we came into the flat terrain of southern Romania. Crossed the blue Danube — better described as the muddy Danube. Circled again, waiting for all elements of the 376th and 98th to get into formation again. The

Danube was an important navigational aid. Navigation in a strange land at high altitude is difficult; but at altitudes of 35 to 50 feet off the ground, and speeds exceeding 200 mph, navigation is almost impossible. Everything goes by blurred. The countryside completely changes every few seconds.

By now a few Liberators had turned back due to different problems. The bombers hit the critical navigation point, the city of Targoviste, and should have headed straight for the final navigational check, the city of Floreste, and then turned south-easterly directly into the city of Ploesti and her five major refineries. The group erred. The ships had turned south-easterly at Targoviste and we were headed for Bucharest, about 50 miles south of Ploesti! Bucharest was headquarters for the German Luftwaffe. By now what little surprise was left had gone. There can be no question about the target as far as the enemy is concerned. Every fighter within flying distance of Ploesti had to be alerted. The battle was soon to commence.

By the time we got reorganized, turned around in a south to north direction and headed up the valley to Ploesti, all hell had broken loose. We were approaching Ploesti from its most guarded area, and it seemed tracer shells of all types were coming from every direction. The battle of Ploesti had begun and it looked like a 'kill or be killed' proposition; the survival of the fittest. Only 11 Liberators had been forced to turn back — 166 made it to Ploesti.

The great ground-air battle began. Haystacks spread open revealing dual-purpose heavy guns: machine-gun nests with heavy ack-ack guns. We were flying just above the tree- and house-tops. The lower to the ground the ships could fly, the safer they seemed to be from the heavy fire. Bomber formations became disorganized dodging barrage balloons, hitting their anchor cables on many occasions. If hit with the propeller the cable would snap, often unbalancing the prop so the engine would have to be feathered. The ship would be forced to drop out of formation, as it could not keep up with only three engines. German fighters would then attack the ship in great numbers, and in a few moments shoot it down. Some ships hit the cables with a section of the wing. Bombers would climb the cable, stall out and crash, or the cable would spin the bomber around causing the ship to go down. Poor devils never had a chance!

Heading north we straddled a freight train, which turned out to be an ack-ack flak train. The tops and sides of cars opened, revealing light and heavy guns. Before bombers could get below levels of gunfire, or any distance from the flak train, we lost about 20 planes. Many bombers were only ten to 20 feet off the ground, flying at speeds in excess of 200 mph.

Little Richard cut two balloon cables with her props, but fortunately we didn't have to feather her engines. The Good Lord was on our side. General Ent and Colonel Compton in *Teggy Ann* were directly off our left wing. The din from the gunfire was like a thousand cannons going off at the same time; machine guns firing constantly. They shot at us with everything — pistols, rifles, machine guns, 20 mm and 30 mm cannons, and the big ack-ack guns. Fighters were cruising just outside the ground-fire perimeter, waiting for a chance to finish us off. By now, some of the ships were dropping their delayed-action bombs. We were tossing out the incendiary sticks and shooting the 50-calibers at the storage tanks and anything that moved. Terrific explosions could be seen and heard in many sections of the oilfields.

Suddenly, all of Ploesti became a mass of fire and smoke. Because of the extremely low altitude of the bombers, many were caught in the concussion and flames of the gigantic gas explosions. Bombers had to tip their wings to keep from hitting the numerous smoke stacks that dotted the area. In just a few seconds, bombers were all over the sky flying every which way, trying to escape the murderous gunfire and gigantic explosions. Bombers were crashing all over the area. Many were flying on only two or three engines. Many were smoking heavily.

The 376th was circling around as we looked for our target. Approaching from south to north instead of west to east complicated matters. The three groups way behind us were now approaching Ploesti from west to east: we were on a collision course with them, and that further complicated the bomber airflow over Ploesti. Everyone was too busy to be scared — time for that if you survive. We were getting the shit shot out of us. Machine guns and flak. Seems we'd been at this for hours. We dropped our 45-second delayed-action 500-pounders on a power house. We couldn't find our assigned target. Blew up many storage tanks.

Just north of Ploesti bombers were regrouping for the long run home. The fighters attacked us from all angles. They tried to dive at the bombers, guns blazing as they swooped underneath us. Several of them hit the ground and exploded. We got down to deck level and fought off the fighters as we headed west. We were practically wing-tip to wing-tip. There was only one word for this — disaster! We had probably lost 70 to 80 planes over the general target area. [Total losses for the mission were in fact 54 ships.]

All of a sudden, the great ground-air battle of Ploesti was over. The critical problem now was gas. One of our bomb-bay tanks was never filled and we were about 400 gallons short. We discussed bailing out before we hit the Adriatic Sea, but decided to take a chance with the ship — even to the point of bellying her into the Med. The immediate problem was to lighten the ship. We tossed out everything that wasn't fastened down. Even tossed out some unused 50-caliber belts, but kept enough to battle the fighters that could intercept us when we reached the Adriatic. The engine mixture was leaned out. Fortunately, when we reached the Adriatic and headed south, we had an extremely heavy tail wind.

We were not intercepted by German

335

fighters from Italian bases. Observed 30 or more large aircraft on an airdrome about 20 miles from Corfu, north-east. The trip over the Med was uneventful. We landed at about 8.00 p.m. — almost 14 hours in the air. Had very little gas left in tanks. The ground personnel were told the target at 12.00 noon, our estimated time of arrival over Ploesti. The ground crew were there to congratulate us. Bombers were crashing into the sea and running out of gas. Almost every returning bomber fired a red flare indicating landing priority — dead or wounded aboard, or mechanical problems. We must have lost 80 to 100 bombers, give or take a few.

The crew all knelt down and kissed the good old solid ground. We had survived Ploesti. The question is, why were we chosen to survive? Bombers were being lost all around us. I remember walking back to the debriefing area and looking up at the sky — millions of blinking stars — and asking the Good Lord, 'Why me? Why was I chosen?' Those who survived Ploesti will never, ever forget it.

The Ploesti mission was a disaster: one third of the ships were lost, around 300 airmen were killed, many more were wounded and scores were taken prisoner.

As Byers wrote, about an hour into the mission the lead ship with the best navigator, Lieutenant Robert W. Wilson, crashed when flying about ten feet above the Mediterranean, broke into two pieces and sank immediately with no survivors. He recalls that the group circled, looking for swimmers, but in fact only one plane circled.

To this day no one who flew the Ploesti mission knows for sure why the ship, Wingo Wango, crashed, although rumours suggest an error by the co-pilot. The Liberator's pilot was Lieutenant Brian Flavelle, a highly-respected pilot who had had vast commercial aviation experience before the war. The plane immediately behind Flavelle's ship on the Ploesti mission was piloted by his friend Second Lieutenant Guy Iovine, carrying the 376th Bomb Group's second best navigator on board, and this was the plane which circled over the wreckage of Flavelle's Liberator to look for survivors. Seeing that there were none, Iovine (who may have been overcome by grief) returned to Benghazi rather than going on to Ploesti, thus depriving the 376th of its number two navigator in addition to losing its best navigator in the crash.

It has been suggested that Iovine's plane was too far behind the other Liberators to catch up, but nevertheless the ship left flying as 'mission leader' carried only a relatively inexperienced navigator. Seeing this, Colonel Compton flying *Teggy Ann*, with General Ent on board, moved up to take over the leader's position. When the bombers reached their critical navigation point over the city of Targoviste, *Teggy Ann* turned in the wrong direction, leading the mission into disaster. After more than 50 years, however, the identity of the person on board *Teggy Ann* who ordered the fatal turn is still unknown.

Richard Dahlstedt, an honourable war veteran who knew both Flavelle and Iovine, commented:

Flavelle was a fine man. Iovine was a different matter; I flew with him several times. In my opinion, and in the light of history, Iovine more than anyone helped destroy the Ploesti mission.

Dahlstedt might also have added that whoever ordered the wrong turn at Targoviste also played a central role in the mission's outcome. Lieutenant Flavelle died on 1 August, 1943, taking with him the reasons for his turn away from the target at Naples during Mission 109 as well as those for his fatal crash into the Mediterranean. Guy Iovine survived the war, but died several years ago with the burden he still carried from the Ploesti mission. Colonel Keith Compton also survived, and lives on with the answers to other questions.

Despite the heavy losses, the vast majority of the airmen who took part in the Ploesti mission survived it, living to fly again and perhaps die on another day. And, as they survived one mission after another, they all undoubtedly hoped that if they were really fortunate they may even survive the war (although, as Dick Byers has already commented, survival sometimes seemed less than appealing: 'Sometimes it would get so cold standing next to the window of a bomber you'd wish you would die — at least then it would be all over.').

But, by the grace of Lady Luck, Byers survived the war, as did most of the flyers mentioned in this book. *Little Richard*, the ship Byers flew on the Ploesti mission, was less fortunate: on 19 August, 1943, when being flown by another crew, the plane was shot down and two of her crew were killed. It was pure chance that *Little Richard* was allocated to another crew that day, and the whims of fortune played an enormous part in allocating life or death to other airmen. Sam Rose, for example, who flew *Lady Be Good* from America to Africa, slipped through the clutches of death's hands twice. In 1942, long before he saw combat, a plane he was piloting from San Francisco to Hawaii lost two engines and crashed near Bay Bridge between Alcatraz and Angel Islands, where it broke in two and sank. In combat, three months after *Lady Be Good* was lost, Rose's Liberator was shot down by ME-109s near Bari. One crewman was killed, but everyone else bailed out safely, including Rose and Jack Hughins (see Chapter 6), who was badly wounded but managed to jump clear.

Luck helped Rose, Hughins and Byers to survive the war, but sadly failed to shine on Bill Hatton and his boys for a handful of days in April, 1943. For, above all, the story of what happened to *Lady Be Good* and her crew can perhaps best be summed up in two words. Rotten luck.

Appendix

The Background to this Book

Lady's Men is the result of considerable research over a period of many years in various parts of America, Britain and beyond. It must be said, however, that thanks to the demanding nature of my work as a fundraising consultant there were often lengthy intervals during which I did no research and the story of *Lady Be Good* was a very long way from my mind.

Lady's Men is, I hope, not too clumsy an attempt to bring into focus the haunting, complex and timeless story of the Liberator B-24D bomber named *Lady Be Good* and the crew who flew the ill-fated ship. The story is one which has fascinated me ever since the discovery of the Liberator by BP employees in 1959, although until recently I entertained no ambition of writing a book on the subject. I remember reading the first major article about the discovery in *Life* magazine a year later. I was working in the film business at the time, co-producing a social documentary film called *Citizen Smith* in New York. I thought then, as I do now, that the story would make a wonderful motion picture and that one day I would participate in its production.

In 1962 Dennis E. McClendon published his book, *Lady Be Good — Mystery Bomber of World War Two*, which I bought and read. I was bewitched. McClendon, a former Second World War pilot, was then a major in the USAF attached to the Pentagon. When he published his work only the surface facts connected with *Lady Be Good* were known: some of the details about the bomber's discovery were vague, and many of the records resulting from the military investigation that followed were hard to come by. But despite this handicap, McClendon wrote an excellent book which accurately reflected what was then known about the Liberator and her crew. He wrote it under pressure in a very brief time, but a full 18 months passed before his publisher finally published.

Even then the first genuine story with substance about *Lady Be Good* and her crew was launched reluctantly.

Dissatisfied with the film business, in 1966 I switched from film-making to fundraising and joined the Community Counselling Service, a prestigious Catholic fundraising company in New York and now the world's largest fundraising firm. They sent me far and wide on scores of assignments all over America, then to England and Ireland. Now and then in the years that followed articles would appear in newspapers and magazines about the enigmatic *Lady Be Good*, and with each one my interest in the subject was rekindled.

In 1982 Dennis McClendon published his book again, this time with an epilogue. New information about *Lady Be Good* had been uncovered; information, I might add, which only deepened the mystery of the aircraft. As before, I bought and read the book and found myself again captivated.

In December, 1983, I was in the remote village of Kadugli, in south central Sudan, producing a film for Irish UNICEF. I had taken a crew of Irish technicians to this village to film the needs of children in that area. The film was later to be shown on television in Ireland and beyond to help stimulate financial support for the children of Sudan. Kadugli, and indeed Sudan, is hot, flat, dusty and, except for the rainy season, as dry as can be. Areas of Sudan are in some ways similar to the spot where the wreckage of *Lady Be Good* rests to this day. This similarity was much on my mind one day as I sat on a prickly straw mat in front of a Kadugli hut, drinking tea with a tall, friendly African whose shiny young skin was more blue than black, and whose brilliant white teeth matched the colour of his immaculate long robe. The similarity prompted me to decide there and then that as soon as possible I would begin work on a *Lady Be Good* film.

The UNICEF film completed, I returned to Dublin. One Saturday afternoon I was visiting a Jesuit friend, Father Jack Brennan, president of University Hall in Hatch Street, and asked if I might use his office phone to call the information operator in Tampa,

Florida. The operator gave me the phone number of Dennis McClendon: a few days later I called McClendon, told him what was on my mind, and he graciously agreed to a meeting in Tampa during my next visit to America. Little did I know that when I called the Tampa operator from University Hall I was sitting only 200 yards away from the head offices of the exploration company Atlantic Resources, whose managing director was Dr Don Sheridan, one of the three BP men who 25 years earlier had located *Lady Be Good* in the Libyan desert.

About a month later, in May, 1984, I flew from New York to Tampa and met the likeable Dennis McClendon. A veteran of the 'big war', he was then a retired US Air Force colonel and a true southern gentleman. Our first meeting lasted many enjoyable hours, and included drinks, dinner and endless talk about *Lady Be Good*. The result of this trip was that Dennis and Len Morgan, who was instrumental in the second publication of McClendon's book, granted me what evolved into an opened-ended option on the book, upon which I would base a screenplay dealing with the *Lady Be Good* story.

It was understood by all that in addition to using Dennis's book for basic information, I would also carry out my own further researches on the subject. These took place over a two-year period, during which time I made it my business to contact the three BP oilmen who had found *Lady Be Good* on the desert floor, Don Sheridan, John Martin and Gordon Bowerman, as well as other BP men connected with the discovery. Each man in his own way was wonderful in providing me with maps, photos, personal recollections and other relevant details.

With the exception of Sheridan, whom I located in Dublin, all the other oilmen connected with the finding of *Lady Be Good* lived either in England or Scotland. I contacted Gordon Bowerman first, in November, 1984, and it took great brilliance on my part to find him. I was in London at the time, so I looked in the London phone book and there he was at Gerald Eve & Co in Savile Row. Gordon was completely unaware that he was listed in the London phone book under his firm's name, so my call was a double surprise to him.

My next step was to find those veterans still living who flew the *Lady Be Good* mission. Luck was on my side when Edwin Gluck, who flew Mission 109, sent me a newspaper article about the former McDonnell-Douglas engineer James Walker and his interest in *Lady Be Good*, which had appeared in the St Louis *Globe-Democrat* in 1979. With the help of the newspaper I traced Walker to Scottsdale, Arizona, and in June, 1985, visited him there for a week. Walker had a long-standing interest in *Lady Be Good*, mainly of a scientific nature thanks to his researches into her engine, but he was also very knowledgeable about other aspects of the aircraft's story. He was good enough to share some of his knowledge with me and I reciprocated by sharing some of mine with him, giving him copies of maps and other information dealing with how *Lady Be Good* was actually found. By then I had gathered many new facts connected with the Liberator's discovery about which few people knew, including details of the actual year and circumstances of the plane's first sighting by British oilmen.

As a result of Walker's interest in the story he had developed links with the 376th Bomb Group's Veterans Association. Quite by chance the association was holding a reunion in October that year, and through Walker an invitation to attend the gathering in San Antonio, Texas, came my way. I had already exchanged letters with a few veterans of the 376th, notable among them being Richard Byers, who had sent me a copy of his book, *Attack*, giving a detailed daily account of his wartime experiences on bombing missions from the Benghazi district.

One of the first men I met at the reunion in October, 1985, was Byers himself, a dynamic and straight-talking veteran of 53 bombing missions. Dick took me under his wing and, with the help of men such as Norman Appold, Dean Lear, Peter Aspasi, Dr Joe Toddonio, Charles Midgley, Harry Heins, Ken DeLong and others, pointed me in the right direction. The veterans helped unlock the past for me with stories, records, maps, and just plain friendship and hospitality. At times it was hard to conceive of these men as the former targets of enemy fighter planes as well as the messengers with bombs, for that is what they all had been. Every man had volunteered for the task, and this for the privilege of putting his life on the line, mission after mission, in those freezing flying crematoria known as Liberators. Many of the veterans in San Antonio had flown Mission 109, and their recollections eventually helped me to assemble the complicated puzzle of *Lady Be Good* — at least insofar as it was possible so many years after the event.

The next three jobs were to write my screenplay, raise the money with which to make the film, and then produce it. By April, 1986, my screenplay was complete, and this was followed by several months of budgeting and other pre-production work which in time suggested that the film would cost ten to 12 million dollars to make. Between 1987 and 1992 I contacted a host of film studios in

America, England and elsewhere for financing. In every case the answer was no. Most had never heard of *Lady Be Good*, and more often than not my screenplay was never read. The same response came from TV companies. I tried the richest man in America: he said 'No'. I tried one of the richest men in England, an American. 'No.' I tried to interest famous directors, but everyone said no and none read the script. Only the great Fred Zinnermann, a giant among directors, responded with a thoughtful letter of regrets and asked not to see the script because mine was not his type of story. Fair enough. I tried approaching young established male film stars through their agents. 'No.'

It was by then June, 1992, and I was having lunch with John Martin, one of *Lady Be Good*'s original finders, in a restaurant in London's Jermyn Street. I hadn't seen John in a few years, and as we ate we were busy catching up on each other's news — and, of course, discussing my financing problems with the film project. As we prepared to leave the restaurant John asked me, 'Have you ever considered writing a new book on *Lady Be Good*? You've done so much research, discovered so many new facts . . . I think you owe it to yourself.'

I don't remember my response to John's suggestion, but I certainly did think about what he said and resolved to see if I could find a publisher willing to consider the idea of a book. I initially tried Macmillan Publishers in London, but they turned me down on the grounds that my subject was too specialized for them. Here we go again, I thought. But Macmillan's Katie Owen, with whom I had been dealing, was kind enough to suggest that I should approach Pen & Sword Books. In rapid order and with a minimum of fuss Leo Cooper said that a more accurate account of *Lady Be Good*'s story could now be told. The result is *Lady's Men*.

Mario Martinez
London, England
August, 1994.

Bibliography

McClendon, Dennis E: *The Lady Be Good*, Mystery Bomber of World War II; 1962 & 1982. John Day, N.Y. & Aero Publishers, Cal, and TAB Books Div, McGraw-Hill Publishing Co., Blue Ridge Summit, Pa., USA. pp: 33, 80, 81, 108, 159, 160.

Barnett, Correlli: *The Desert Generals*. Ref: the UK 1983 Pan edition: 233, 234. Dmitri, Ivan: *Flight to Everywhere*. USA, 1944, Whittlesey House/McGraw-Hill. A series of photographs with accompanying narrative by author. pp: 113, 119.

Hart, Liddell B. H.: *History of the Second World War*, 1970, Cassell, London, UK.

R. Ernest Dupuy and Trevor Dupuy: *The Encyclopedia of Military History*; 1970. Harper & Row Publishers, N.Y. & London.

Self-published book:
Byers, Richard G. (T/Sgt): *Attack*, 1984, Apollo Books, Inc. Winona, Minnesota, USA. Available in UK for ref at RAF Museum, Hendon. A series of WW II diary entries from 1943. pp: 22, 30, 36, 37, 38, 39, 174, 175, 176, 181, 182, 183, 184, 185, 186.

Other Information Sources

Magazines:
LIFE, March 7, 1960.
AFTER THE BATTLE, 25th issue, 1979.
SAGA, February, 1960.
THE RETIRED OFFICER, September 1977
CIRCA, 1979.

Unpublished Stories and Diaries of 376th BG veterans:
BENGHAZI NIGHTS, Kenneth R. DeLong, Brandon, Florida
4/4/43 diary entry of William Goode, Jacksonville, Florida
4/4/43 diary entry of Jack Hughins, Odessa, Texas
MILITARY RECORD OF SAMUEL DAWSON ROSE, S. M. Rose, Visalia, Cal.

Other 376th BG veterans:
Norman C.   Gainesville, Georgia
Appold

Peter Aspasi	Woburn, Massachusetts
James O. Britt	San Diego, California
Richard G. Byers	Bella Vista, Arkansas
Dr Dean A. Christie	Oceanside, California (R.I.P.)
James R. Cooke	Danville, Kentucky
Richard R. Dahlstedt	Beach Haven Gardens, N.J.
Joseph S. Domino	Pittsburgh, Pennsylvania
Homer Drake	Ft. Lauderdale, Florida
George W. Garrett	Hamilton, Georgia
Wiley L. Golden	Cincinnati, Ohio (R.I.P.)
Edwin L. Gluck	Pittsburgh, Pennsylvania
Richard F. Hurd	Plainfield, Vermont
Harry L. Heins	Ventura, California
Dean E. Lear	Mesa, Arizona
William M. McCain	Rancho Mirage, California
Louis R. Nichols	Billings, Montana
Charles 'Holley' Midgley	Mobile, Alabama
William M. Poynter	Covina, California
John Susmuth	Old Tappan, N.J.
Thomas Shumaker	San Diego, California
Dr Joe Toddonio	Saugus, Massachusetts

Williard Tressler   Hico, Texas
Paul T. Wagner   Boulder City, Nevada

99th BG veteran:
George F. Coen   Albuquerque, New
                Mexico

Oilmen: (British & Irish)
F. Gordon   Somerset, England
Bowerman
David W. Glover Aberdeen, Scotland
Charles P.   Hampshire, England
Hellewell
Ken W. Honey   Cornwall, England
Don G.   Essex, England
Livingstone
Dr A. John Martin Norfolk, England
Ronald G.   Edinburgh, Scotland
MacLean
Dr Don J. R.   Dublin, Ireland
Sheridan
Richard M.   Surrey, England
'Slinger' Woods

Others who contributed:
Mrs Elizabeth Betty Henry USA (R.I.P.)
Paul J. Henry   USA
James W. Walker   USA

David Clarke   Scotland
Austin Farina   England
Frederick Flower   England
V. Rev. Martin Bennett   England
V. Rev. John Brennan S.J.   Ireland
Mrs Vivian McClendon   USA (R.I.P.)
Dennis E. McClendon   USA
Len A. G. Morgan   USA
Francis X. Hatton   USA (R.I.P.)
Geoff Hill   England
Mrs Joyce Pope   England
Len Woodgate   England
Group Capt. R. Randall   England
Michael Stewart (MoD)   England
Frances Sito   England
Dr Roberto Terlevich   England/
                                 Argentina
Dr Gillian Gibbs   England
Adolph P. 'Zeke' Zeleny   England

Examples of Newspapers:
Libya's Sunday Ghibli News, June 1959.
The Tripoli Mirror, May 1959.
'Perspective', The St Louis Globe
    Democrat, 21, November 1974.
The Cleveland Plain Dealer, July 26, 1959.
Sunday Metro, The Las Vegas Sun,
    April 21, 1985.

New York Herald Tribune, 19, August
1962. And others.

Publications and Television:
THE NINTH AIR FORCE, Aero
Publishers, Inc.
THE LOG OF THE LIBERATORS,
Aero Publishers, Inc. 1973
THE B-24 LIBERATOR, Arco
Publishing Co.
CBS's Armstrong Circle Theatre,
2 February, 1960.

Documents:
a. The Fuller/Need report, 1959.
b. THE RAF 'Report Of Desert Rescue
Exercise', by Flt. Lt. B. Sellers, 1968.
c. USAF special orders May – October
1942.
d. LBG's 'Radio Data' sheets.
e. LBG's 'Navigator's Log'.
f. LBG's desert escape map reproduction.
g. Sheridan/Martin/Bowerman maps
dealing with LBG's discovery.
h. British (L.R.D.G.) map of desert plain.
i. Photographs.
j. Sorte reports of section B Mission 109
returning pilots.

k. Extract from Operational Summary No. 43, 4 April 1943 from Headquarters NW African Air Force regarding B-17's mission to Naples.
l. USAF special orders dealing with 1st Lt. William J. Hatton, May – October 1942.
m. Correspondence (1941 – 43) between William J. Hatton and his parents and between US War Department and his parents or other relatives, (1943 – 1960).
n. Telegraphic message from Soluch to Benghazi, 5 April, 1943.

Associations And Museums:
376th Bomb Group Veterans Association.
99th Bomb Group Historical Society.
RAF Museum, Hendon, England
RAF Museum, Cosford, Wolverhampton, England
Imperial War Museum, London, England
Museum of Natural History, London, England
Greenwich Observatory, England

Companies:
The British Petroleum Oil Company

FATAL RING OF LIGHT
Helen Eastwood

Katy's brother was supposed to have died in 1897 but a scrawled note in his handwriting showed July 1899. What had happened to him in those two years? Katy was determined to help him.

NIGHT ACTION
Alan Evans

Captain David Brent sails at dead of night to the German occupied Normandy town of St. Jean on a mission which will stretch loyalty and ingenuity to its limits, and beyond.

A MURDER TOO MANY
Elizabeth Ferrars

Many, including the murdered man's widow, believed the wrong man had been convicted. The further murder of a key witness in the earlier case convinced Basnett that the seemingly unrelated deaths were linked.

THE WILDERNESS WALK
Sheila Bishop

Stifling unpleasant memories of a misbegotten romance in Cleave with Lord Francis Aubrey, Lavinia goes on holiday there with her sister. The two women are thrust into a romantic intrigue involving none other than Lord Francis.

THE RELUCTANT GUEST
Rosalind Brett

Ann Calvert went to spend a month on a South African farm with Theo Borland and his sister. They both proved to be different from her first idea of them, and there was Storr Peterson — the most disturbing man she had ever met.

ONE ENCHANTED SUMMER
Anne Tedlock Brooks

A tale of mystery and romance and a girl who found both during one enchanted summer.

CLOUD OVER MALVERTON
Nancy Buckingham

Dulcie soon realises that something is seriously wrong at Malverton, and when violence strikes she is horrified to find herself under suspicion of murder.

AFTER THOUGHTS
Max Bygraves

The Cockney entertainer tells stories of his East End childhood, of his RAF days, and his post-war showbusiness successes and friendships with fellow comedians.

MOONLIGHT
AND MARCH ROSES
D. Y. Cameron

Lynn's search to trace a missing girl takes her to Spain, where she meets Clive Hendon. While untangling the situation, she untangles her emotions and decides on her own future.

NURSE ALICE IN LOVE
Theresa Charles

Accepting the post of nurse to little Fernie Sherrod, Alice Everton could not guess at the romance, suspense and danger which lay ahead at the Sherrod's isolated estate.

POIROT INVESTIGATES
Agatha Christie

Two things bind these eleven stories together — the brilliance and uncanny skill of the diminutive Belgian detective, and the stupidity of his Watson-like partner, Captain Hastings.

LET LOOSE THE TIGERS
Josephine Cox

Queenie promised to find the long-lost son of the frail, elderly murderess, Hannah Jason. But her enquiries threatened to unlock the cage where crucial secrets had long been held captive.

THE TWILIGHT MAN
Frank Gruber

Jim Rand lives alone in the California desert awaiting death. Into his hermit existence comes a teenage girl who blows both his past and his brief future wide open.

DOG IN THE DARK
Gerald Hammond

Jim Cunningham breeds and trains gun dogs, and his antagonism towards the devotees of show spaniels earns him many enemies. So when one of them is found murdered, the police are on his doorstep within hours.

THE RED KNIGHT
Geoffrey Moxon

When he finds himself a pawn on the chessboard of international espionage with his family in constant danger, Guy Trent becomes embroiled in moves and countermoves which may mean life or death for Western scientists.

TIGER TIGER
Frank Ryan

A young man involved in drugs is found murdered. This is the first event which will draw Detective Inspector Sandy Woodings into a whirlpool of murder and deceit.

CAROLINE MINUSCULE
Andrew Taylor

Caroline Minuscule, a medieval script, is the first clue to the whereabouts of a cache of diamonds. The search becomes a deadly kind of fairy story in which several murders have an other-worldly quality.

LONG CHAIN OF DEATH
Sarah Wolf

During the Second World War four American teenagers from the same town join the Army together. Forty-two years later, the son of one of the soldiers realises that someone is systematically wiping out the families of the four men.

THE LISTERDALE MYSTERY
Agatha Christie

Twelve short stories ranging from the light-hearted to the macabre, diverse mysteries ingeniously and plausibly contrived and convincingly unravelled.

TO BE LOVED
Lynne Collins

Andrew married the woman he had always loved despite the knowledge that Sarah married him for reasons of her own. So much heartache could have been avoided if only he had known how vital it was to be loved.

ACCUSED NURSE
Jane Converse

Paula found herself accused of a crime which could cost her her job, her nurse's reputation, and even the man she loved, unless the truth came to light.

BUTTERFLY MONTANE
Dorothy Cork

Parma had come to New Guinea to marry Alec Rivers, but she found him completely disinterested and that overbearing Pierce Adams getting entirely the wrong idea about her.

HONOURABLE FRIENDS
Janet Daley

Priscilla Burford is happily married when she meets Junior Environment Minister Alistair Thurston. Inevitably, sexual obsession and political necessity collide.

WANDERING MINSTRELS
Mary Delorme

Stella Wade's career as a concert pianist might have been ruined by the rudeness of a famous conductor, so it seemed to her agent and benefactor. Even Sir Nicholas fails to see the possibilities when John Tallis falls deeply in love with Stella.

CHATEAU OF FLOWERS
Margaret Rome

Alain, Comte de Treville needed a wife to look after him, and Fleur went into marriage on a business basis only, hoping that eventually he would come to trust and care for her.

CRISS-CROSS
Alan Scholefield

As her ex-husband had succeeded in kidnapping their young daughter once, Jane was determined to take her safely back to England. But all too soon Jane is caught up in a new web of intrigue.

DEAD BY MORNING
Dorothy Simpson

Leo Martindale's body was discovered outside the gates of his ancestral home. Is it, as Inspector Thanet begins to suspect, murder?